# THE YANKEE PROBLEM

Produced in the Republic of South Carolina by

SHOTWELL PUBLISHING LLC
Post Office Box 2592
Columbia, South Carolina 29202

www.ShotwellPublishing.com

ISBN-13: 978-0692733905
ISBN- 0692733906

10 9 8 7 6 5 4 3 2 1

# THE YANKEE
# PROBLEM

## An American Dilemma

## Clyde N. Wilson

---

The Wilson Files I

---

SHOTWELL · COLUMBIA · So. CAR. · EST. 2015 · PUBLISHING

# Comments on Clyde Wilson

---

*Clyde Wilson had been ploughing the ground long before many of us came to plant.*
— Donald Livingston

*Clyde Wilson is a national treasure.*
— Alice Teller

*My Granddaddy writes a lot.*
— Adam V. Smith

*Clyde Wilson shows great ability in the field of intellectual history.*
— American Historical Review

*Clyde Wilson exhibits the rarest kind of courage---intellectual courage.*
— Columbia, SC, State

*Clyde Wilson is certainly the biggest intellectual heavyweight with the neo-Confederate scene.*
— Southern Poverty Law Center

*It seems you take Sherman's March as a personal affront. Good. The South started the REBELLION and we finished it.*
— Anonymous e-mail

*... a careful scholar who has thought hard and deep about his beloved South. Wilson is, in short, an exemplary historian who displays formidable talent.*
— Eugene Genovese

*... lucid prose and sharp analysis.*
— Blue and Gray Magazine.

*I have long been waiting for a collection of Wilson's essays, and, having seen it, I can say that it is well worth careful and repeated reading.*
— Joseph Stromberg

*. . . a mind as precise and expansive as an encyclopedia ... These are the same old preoccupations given new life and meaning by a real mind---as opposed to what passes for minds in the current intellectual establishment.*
— Thomas H. Landess

*This generous collection of Clyde Wilson's essays ... places him on the same level with all the unreconstructed greats in modern Southern letters: Donald Davidson, Andrew Lytle, Frank L. Owsley, Richard Weaver, and M.E. Bradford.*
— Joseph Scotchie

*The silver-tongued voice of the New Right.*
— Chilton Williamson, National Review

*Clyde Wilson is an obstreperous soldier in the great Jacobin wars that have plagued the nation.*
— Robert C. Cheeks

*Professor Clyde N. Wilson's latest book is remarkable in many ways. At one and the same time it is richly variegated and philosophically sound, while its style and form are consistently elegant.*
— Jack Kershaw

*It would be both wise and chastening to read this entire masterly volume, which presents a rare and enlightened view of both our perils and our opportunities.*
— Otto Scott

*He likes hanging around grave yards and reading tombstones.*
— Ex-wife

*You, Sir, are obviously educated far beyond your intelligence. I now suppose that the University of South Carolina is also a hotbed of communist inspired anti war, anti American hatred.*
—S. Miller, N.J.

# CONTENTS

# Preface

American historians and commentators have long strained to explain why the South was such a peculiar deviation from the American mainstream that it had to be put down by force. About thirty years ago I suggested that they were asking the wrong question. It was the North that needed studying. It was the North that had changed radically in the antebellum era and brought on the War Between the States. The proper study for historians, I wrote, was Northern history. In recent years a fair amount of scholarly literature has appeared that addresses that question, but there is still much more to be learned.

Versions of some of these essays have appeared previously in *Chronicles, Confederate Veteran,* www.abbevilleinstitute.org, and www.lewrockwell.com. There is some repetition but things that are so important and neglected in the understanding of American history cannot be said too often.

Clyde N. Wilson
Dutch Fork, South Carolina, 2016

# The Yankee Problem in American History

*It is true we are completely under the saddle of Massachusetts and Connecticut,
and that they ride us very hard, cruelly insulting our feelings, as well as exhausting
our strength and substance.*
—Thomas Jefferson, 1798

*There is at work in this land a Yankee spirit and an American spirit.*
—James H. Thornwell, 1859

———————

SINCE THE 2000 PRESIDENTIAL ELECTION, much attention has
been paid to a map showing the sharp geographical division between the
two candidates' support. Gore prevailed in the power and plunder-seeking
Deep North (Northeast, Upper Midwest, Pacific Coast) and Bush in the
regions inhabited by productive and decent Americans. There is nothing new
about this. Historically speaking, it is just one more manifestation of the
Yankee problem.

Scholars are at last starting to pay some attention to one of the most
important and most neglected subjects in United States history — the Yankee
problem.*

By Yankee I do not mean everybody from north of the Potomac and
Ohio. Lots of them have always been good folks. The firemen who died in
the World Trade Center on September 11 were Americans. The politicians
and TV personalities who stood around telling us what we are to think about
it are Yankees. I am using the term historically to designate that peculiar
ethnic group descended from New Englanders, who can be easily recognized
by their arrogance, hypocrisy, greed, lack of congeniality, and penchant for
ordering other people around. Puritans long ago abandoned anything that
might be good in their religion but have never given up the notion that they

1

are the chosen saints whose mission is to make America, and the world, into the perfection of their own image.

Hillary Rodham Clinton, raised a Northern Methodist in Chicago, is a museum-quality specimen of the Yankee — self-righteous, ruthless, and self-aggrandizing. Northern Methodism and Chicago were both, in their formative periods, hotbeds of abolitionist, high tariff Black Republicanism. The Yankee temperament, it should be noted, makes a neat fit with the Stalinism that was brought into the Deep North by later immigrants.

The ethnic division between Yankees and other Americans goes back to earliest colonial times. Up until the War for Southern Independence, Southerners were considered to be the American mainstream and Yankees were considered to be the "peculiar" people. Because of a long campaign of cultural imperialism and the successful military imperialism engineered by the Yankees since the war, the South has been considered the problem, the deviation from the true American norm. Historians have made an industry of explaining why the South is different (and evil, for that which defies the "American" as now established, is by definition evil). Is the South different because of slavery? White supremacy? The climate? Pellagra? Illiteracy? Poverty? Guilt? Defeat? Celtic wildness rather than Anglo-Saxon sobriety?

Unnoticed in all this literature was a hidden assumption: the North is normal, the standard of all things American, and good. Anything that does not conform is a problem to be explained and a condition to be annihilated. What about that hidden assumption? Should not historians be interested in understanding how the North got to be the way it is? Indeed, is there any question in American history more important?

According to standard accounts of American history (*i.e.*, Northern mythology), New Englanders fought the Revolution and founded glorious American freedom as had been planned by the "Puritan Fathers." Southerners, who had always been of questionable character, because of their fanatic devotion to slavery, wickedly rebelled against government of, by, and for the people, were put down by the armies of the Lord, and should be ever grateful for not having been exterminated. (This is clearly the view of the anonymous Union Leaguer from Portland, Maine, who recently sent me a chamber pot labelled "Robert E. Lee's soup tureen.") And out of their benevolence and devotion to the ideal of freedom, the North struck the chains from the suffering black people. (They should be forever grateful, also. Take a look at the Boston statue with happy blacks adoring the feet of Col. Robert Gould Shaw.)

Aside from the fact that every generalization in this standard history is false, an obvious defect in it is that, for anyone familiar with American history before the War, it is clear that "Southern" was American and Yankees were the problem. America was Washington and Jefferson, the Louisiana Purchase and the Battle of New Orleans, John Randolph and Henry Clay, Daniel Morgan, Daniel Boone, and Francis Marion. Southerners had made the Constitution, saved it under Jefferson from the Yankees, fought the wars, acquired the territory, and settled the West, including the Northwest. To most Americans, in Pennsylvania and Indiana as well as Virginia and Georgia, this was a basic view up until about 1850. New England had been a threat, a nuisance, and a negative force in the progress of America. Northerners, including some patriotic New Englanders, believed this as much as Southerners.

When Washington Irving, whose family were among the early Anglo-Dutch settlers of New York, wrote the story about the "Headless Horseman," he was ridiculing Yankees. The prig Ichabod Crane had come over from Connecticut and made himself a nuisance. So a young man (New York young men were then normal young men rather than Yankees) played a trick on him and sent him fleeing back to Yankeeland where he belonged. James Fenimore Cooper, of another early New York family, felt the same way about New Englanders, who appear unfavourably in his writings. Yet another New York writer, James Kirke Paulding (among many others) wrote a book defending the South and attacking abolitionists. It is not unreasonable to conclude that in *Moby Dick*, the New York Democrat Herman Melville modeled the fanatical Captain Ahab on the Yankee abolitionist. In fact, the term "Yankee" appears to originate in some mingling of Dutch and Indian words, to designate New Englanders. Obviously, both the Dutch New Yorkers and the Native Americans recognized them as "different."

Young Abe Lincoln amused his neighbours in southern Indiana and Illinois, nearly all of whom, like his own family, had come from the South, with "Yankee jokes," stories making fun of dishonest peddlers from New England. They were the most popular stories in his repertoire, except for the dirty ones.

Right into the war, Northerners opposed to the conquest of the South blamed the conflict on fanatical New Englanders out for power and plunder, not on the good Americans in the South who had been provoked beyond bearing.

Many people, and not only in the South, thought that Southerners, according to their nature, had been loyal to the Union, had served it, fought and sacrificed for it as long as they could. New Englanders, according to their nature, had always been grasping for themselves while proclaiming their righteousness and superiority.

The Yankees succeeded so well, by the long cultural war described in these volumes, and by the North's military victory, that there was no longer a Yankee problem. Now the Yankee was America and the South was the problem. America, the Yankee version, was all that was normal and right and good. Southerners understood who had won the war (not Northerners, though they had shed a lot of blood, but the accursed Yankees.) With some justification they began to regard all Northerners as Yankees, even the hordes of foreigners who had been hired to wear the blue.

Here is something closer to a real history of the United States: American freedom was not a legacy of the "Puritan Fathers," but of Virginians who proclaimed and spread constitutional rights. New England gets some credit for beginning the War of Independence. After the first few years, however, Yankees played little part. The war was fought and won in the South. Besides, New Englanders had good reasons for independence — they did not fit into the British Empire economically, since one of their main industries was smuggling, and the influential Puritan clergy hated the Church of England. Southerners, in fighting for independence, were actually going against their economic interests for the sake of principle.

# The Yankee Problem

Once Southerners had gone into the Union (which a number of wise statesmen like Patrick Henry and George Mason warned them against), the Yankees began to show how they regarded the new federal government: as an instrument to be used for their own purposes. Southerners long continued to view the Union as a vehicle for mutual cooperation, as they often naively still do.

In the first Congress, Yankees demanded that the federal government continue the British subsidies to their fishing fleets. While Virginia and the other Southern states gave up their vast western lands for future new states, New Englanders demanded a special preserve for themselves (the "Western Reserve" in Ohio).

Under John Adams, the New England quest for power grew into a frenzy. They passed the Sedition Law to punish anti-government words (as long as they controlled the government) in clear violation of the Constitution. During the election of 1800 the preachers in New England told their congregations that Thomas Jefferson was a French Jacobin who would set up the guillotine in their town squares and declare women common property. (What else could be expected from a dissolute slaveholder?) In fact, Jefferson's well-known distaste for mixing of church and state rested largely on his dislike of the power of the New England self-appointed saints.

When Jeffersonians took power, the New Englanders fought them with all their diminishing strength. Their poet William Cullen Bryant regarded the Louisiana Purchase as nothing but a large swamp for Jefferson to pursue his atheistic penchant for science.

The War of 1812, the Second War of Independence, was decisive for the seemingly permanent discrediting of New England. The Yankee ruling class opposed the war even though it was begun by Southerners on behalf of oppressed American seamen, most of whom were New Englanders. Yankees did not care about their oppressed poorer citizens because they were making big bucks smuggling into wartime Europe. One New England congressman attacked young patriot John C. Calhoun as a backwoodsman who had never seen a sail and who was unqualified to deal with foreign policy.

During the war Yankees traded with the enemy and talked openly of secession. (Southerners *never* spoke of secession in time of war.) Massachusetts refused to have its militia called into constitutional federal service even after invasion, and then, notoriously for years after, demanded that the federal government pay its militia expenses.

Historians have endlessly repeated that the "Era of Good Feelings" under President Monroe refers to the absence of party strife. Actually, the term was first used to describe the state of affairs in which New England traitorousness had declined to the point that a Virginia president could visit Boston without being mobbed.

Yankee political arrogance was soul-mate to Yankee cultural arrogance. Throughout the antebellum period, New England literature was characterized and promoted as *the* American literature, and non-Yankee writers, in most cases much more talented and original, were ignored or slandered. Edgar Allan Poe had great fun ridiculing the literary pretensions of New Englanders, but they largely succeeded in dominating the idea of American literature into the 20th century. Generations of Americans have been cured of reading forever by being forced to digest dreary third-string New England poets as "American literature."

In 1789, a Connecticut Puritan preacher named Jedidiah Morse published the first book of *American Geography*. The trouble was, it was not an American geography but a Yankee geography. Most of the book was taken up with describing the virtues of New England. Once you got west of the Hudson River, as Morse saw it and conveyed to the world's reading public, the U.S. was a benighted land inhabited by lazy, dirty Scotch-Irish and Germans in the Middle States and lazy, morally depraved Southerners, corrupted and enervated by slavery. New Englanders were pure Anglo-Saxons with all virtues. The rest of the Americans were questionable people of lower or mongrel ancestry. The theme of New Englanders as pure Anglo-Saxons continued right down through the 20th century. The alleged saints of American equality operated on a theory of their racial superiority. While Catholics and Jews were, in the South, accepted and loyal Southerners, Yankees burned down convents and banished Jews from the Union Army lines.

A few years after Morse, Noah Webster, also from Connecticut, published his *American Dictionary* and *American Spelling Book*. The trouble was, it was not an American dictionary but a New England dictionary. As Webster declared in his preface, New Englanders spoke and spelled the purest and best form of English of any people in the *world*. Southerners and others ignored Webster and spelled and pronounced real English until after the War of Southern Independence.

Yankees after the War of 1812 were acutely aware of their minority status. And here is the important point: they launched a deliberate campaign to take over control of the idea of "America."

The campaign was multi-faceted. Politically, they gained profits from the protective tariff and from legislation. This is nothing new in human history. But the New England greed was marked by its peculiar assumptions of moral superiority. New Englanders, who were selling their products in a market from which competition had been excluded by the tariff, proclaimed that the low price of cotton was due to the fact that Southerners lacked the drive and enterprise of virtuous Yankees! (When the South was actually the *productive* part of the U.S. economy.)

This transfer of wealth built the strength of the North. It was even more profitable than the slave trade (which New England shippers carried on from Africa to Brazil and Cuba right up to the War Between the States) and the Chinese opium trade (which they were also to break into).

Another phase of the Yankee campaign for what they considered their rightful dominance was the capture of the history of the American Revolution. At a time when decent Americans celebrated the Revolution as the common glory of all, New Englanders were publishing a literature claiming the whole credit for themselves. A scribbler from Maine named Lorenzo Sabine, for one example among many, published a book in which he claimed that the Revolution in the South had been won by New England soldiers because Southerners were traitorous and enervated by slavery. As William Gilmore Simms pointed out, it was all lies. When Daniel Webster was received hospitably in Charleston, he made a speech in which he commemorated the graves of the many heroic Revolutionary soldiers from

New England which were to be found in the South. The trouble was, those graves did not exist. Many Southern volunteers had fought in the North, but no soldier from north of Pennsylvania (except a few generals) had ever fought in the South!

George Washington was a bit of a problem here, so the honour-driven, foxhunting Virginia gentleman was transformed by phony folklore into a prim New Englander in character, a false image that has misled and repulsed countless Americans since.

It should be clear; this was not merely misplaced pride. It was a deliberate, systematic effort by the Massachusetts elite to take control of American symbols and disparage all competing claims.

Another successful effort was a New England claim on the West. When New Englanders referred to "the West" in antebellum times, they meant the parts of Ohio and adjacent states settled by New Englanders. The rest of the great American West did not count. In fact, the great drama of danger and adventure and achievement that was the American West, from the Appalachians to the Pacific, was predominantly the work of Southerners and not of New Englanders at all. In the Midwest, the New Englanders came after Southerners had tamed the wilderness, and they looked down upon the early settlers. But in Western movies we still have the inevitable family from Boston moving west by covered wagon. Such a thing never existed! The people moving west in covered wagons were from the upper South and were despised by Boston.

So our West is reduced, in literature, to *The Oregon Trail*, a silly book written by a Boston tourist, and the phony cavortings of the Eastern sissy Teddy Roosevelt in the cattle country opened by Southerners. And the great American outdoors is now symbolized by Henry David Thoreau and a little frog pond at Walden, in sight of the Boston smokestacks. The Pennsylvanian Owen Wister knew better when he entitled his Wyoming novel *The Virginian*.

To fully understand what the Yankee is today — builder of the all-powerful "multicultural" therapeutic state (with himself giving the orders and collecting the rewards) which is the perfection of history and which is to be exported to all peoples, by guided missiles on women and children if necessary — we need a bit more real history.

That history is philosophical, or rather theological, and demographic. New Englanders lived in a barren land. Some of their surplus sons went to sea. Many others moved west when it was safe to do so. By 1830, half the people in the state of New York were New England-born. By 1850, New Englanders had tipped the political balance in the Midwest, with the help of German revolutionaries and authoritarians who had flooded in after the 1848 revolutions.

The leading editors in New York City, Horace Greeley and William Cullen Bryant, and the big money men, were New England-born. Thaddeus Stevens, the Pennsylvania steel tycoon and Radical Republican, was from Vermont. (Thanks to the tariff, he made $6,000 extra profit on every mile of railroad rails he sold.)

The North had been Yankeeized, for the most part quietly, by control of churches, schools, and other cultural institutions, and by whipping up a frenzy of paranoia about the alleged plot of the South to *spread slavery to the North*, which was as imaginary as Jefferson's guillotine.

The people that Cooper and Irving had despised as interlopers now controlled New York! The Yankees could now carry a majority in the North and in 1860 elect the first sectional president in U.S. history — a threat to the South to knuckle under or else. In time, even the despised Irish Catholics began to think like Yankees.

We must also take note of the intellectual revolution amongst the Yankees which created the modern version of self-righteous authoritarian "Liberalism" so well exemplified by Mrs. Clinton. In the 1830s, Ralph Waldo Emerson went to Germany to study. There he learned from philosophers that the world was advancing by dialectical process to an ever-higher state. He returned to Boston, and after marrying the dying daughter of a banker, resigned from the clergy, declared the sacraments to be a remnant of barbarism, and proclaimed The American as the "New Man" who was leaving behind the garbage of the past and blazing the way into the future state of perfection for humanity. Emerson has ever since in many quarters been regarded as *the* American philosopher, the true interpreter of the meaning of America.

From the point of view of Christianity, this "American" doctrine is heresy. From the point of view of history, it is nonsense. But it is powerful enough for Ronald Reagan, who should have known better, to proclaim America as the shining City upon a Hill that was to redeem mankind. And powerful enough that the United States has long pursued a bipartisan foreign policy, one of the guiding assumptions of which is that America is the model of perfection to which all the world should want to conform.

The highflying Yankee rhetoric of Emerson and Hillary Rodham Clinton has a nether side, which has its historical origins in the "Burnt Over District." The "Burnt Over District" was well known to antebellum Americans. Emersonian notions bore strange fruit in the central regions of New York State settled by the overflow of poorer Yankees from New England. It was "Burnt Over" because it (along with a similar area in northern Ohio) was swept over time and again by post-millennial revivalism. Here preachers like Charles G. Finney began to confuse Emerson's future state of perfection with Christianity, and God's plan for humanity with American chosenness.

If this were true, then anything that stood in the way of American perfection must be eradicated. The threatening evil at various times was liquor, tobacco, the Catholic Church, the Masonic order, meat-eating, marriage. Within the small area of the Burnt Over District and within the space of a few decades was generated what historians have misnamed the "Jacksonian reform movement:" Joseph Smith received the *Book of Mormon* from the Angel Moroni; William Miller began the Seventh Day Adventists by predicting, inaccurately, the end of the world; the free love colony of John Humphrey Noyes flourished at Oneida; the first feminist convention was held at Seneca Falls; and John Brown, who was born in Connecticut, collected accomplices and financial backers for his mass murder expeditions.

# The Yankee Problem

It was in this milieu that abolitionism, as opposed to the antislavery sentiment shared by many Americans, including Southerners, had its origins. Abolitionism, despite what has been said later, was *not* based on sympathy for the black people nor on an ideal of natural rights. It was based on the hysterical conviction that Southern slaveholders were evil sinners who stood in the way of fulfilment of America's divine mission to establish Heaven on Earth. It was not the Union that our Southern forefathers seceded from, but the deadly combination of Yankee greed and righteousness.

Most abolitionists had little knowledge of or interest in black people or knowledge of life in the South. Slavery promoted *sin* and thus must end. No thought was given to what would happen to the African-Americans. In fact, many abolitionists expected that evil Southern whites and blacks would disappear and the land be repopulated by virtuous Yankees.

The darker side of the Yankee mind has had its expression in American history as well as the side of high ideals. Timothy McVeigh from New York and the Unabomber from Harvard are, like John Brown, examples of this side of the Yankee problem. (Even though distinguished Yankee intellectuals have declared that their violence was a product of the evil "Southern gun culture.")

General Richard Taylor, in one of the best Confederate memoirs, *Destruction and Reconstruction*, related what happened as he surrendered the last Confederate troops east of the Mississippi in 1865. A German, wearing the uniform of a Yankee general and speaking in heavily accented English, lectured him that now that the war was over, Southerners would be taught "the true American principles." Taylor replied, sardonically, that he regretted that his grandfather, an officer in the Revolution, and his father, President of the United States, had not passed on to him true American principles. Yankeeism was triumphant.

Since the Confederate surrender, the Yankee has always been a strong and often dominant force in American society, though occasionally tempered by Southerners and other representatives of Western civilization in America. In the 1960s the Yankee had one of his periodic eruptions of mania such as he had in the 1850s. Since then, he has managed to destroy a good part of the liberty and morals of the American peoples. It remains to be seen whether his conquest is permanent or whether in the future we may be, at least to some degree, emancipated from it.

---

*See Susan-Mary Grant, *North over South*; Harlow W. Sheidley, *Sectional Nationalism*; Richard F. Bensel, *Yankee Leviathan*; Ernest L. Tuveson, *Redeemer Nation*; Marc Egnal, *Clash of Extremes*; Thomas Fleming, *A Disease in the Public Mind.*; Anne Norton, *Alternative Americas*; Heather Cox Richardson, *The Greatest Nation on Earth*.

# The Yankee Problem, Again

S INCE THE 2004 ELECTION, the media have been full of observations about the United States being two countries with different ideas and values — the blue (Kerry) and red (Bush) states. Some of the Blues (northeast, upper Midwest, and their colonies on the Pacific) have even been talking about secession from us ignorant bigots who inhabit the Heartland and South.

If the people who run and staff the media knew any American history, which they don't, they would know that there is nothing new about all of this. The Blue regions are simply the domain of the Yankees. Astute readers will remember that I explained it all previously in "The Yankee Problem in American History."

In that article I pointed out that Yankees are a type produced by the Deep North who have been marked throughout American history by their greed, hypocrisy, fanaticism, and desire to lord it over the rest of us Americans – politically, economically, and culturally.

Thomas Jefferson pointed to the phenomenon of the Yankee just before his election as president when he wrote: "It is true that we are completely under the saddle of Massachusetts and Connecticut, and that they ride us very hard, insulting our feelings, as well as exhausting our strength and substance." At about the same time he remarked of New England, the original breeding ground of Yankees, that they were "marked with such a perversity of character" that the natural political division of the United States would always be between Americans (non-Yankees) and Yankees.

There is nothing new about Yankees threatening secession either. Twice during the administrations of Jefferson and Madison, and several times later, they threatened to break up the Union in fits of pique when they failed to get their way. The current Blue commentators are using extreme language to

13

characterize the non-Kerry states. To hear them tell it, the red states are dominated by religious maniacs and militarists – *i.e.*, people who actually believe the Bible and love their country. There is nothing new about this invective either. This kind of hateful demonization of those who resist domination by Yankees has been commonplace for about three hundred years or more.

And, of course, the South, being the biggest obstacle to Yankee domination, has always been the major recipient of Yankee slander and hate. (I can never forget the pundit who blamed the crimes of Timothy McVeigh and the Unabomber on "the Southern gun culture.") This hateful rhetoric was used in the past and is now used to abuse Dixie for giving the essential winning margin to the Republicans (something which, in the light of Southern history, is in itself a bizarre development).

I can't see that the Blues really have anything to complain about. They already own the store – lock, stock, and barrel. Nobody with the least sense could detect any meaningful difference between Bush and Kerry. Bush is as likely to do something about "moral values" as his father was to follow through on "no new taxes." It takes a pretty short memory not to have figured out by now that the Bushes are Yankees through and through and that what they say to get elected and what they do are two unrelated things.

Southerners were given a choice between a weird rich boy from Connecticut and an even weirder rich boy from Massachusetts and we picked the former, who at least did not come flat out for sodomy and treason. (Besides, the Massachusetts boy is descended from Yankee slave traders, the Forbes family, people who have never been popular in the South.)

Throughout the 20th century Yankees browbeat Southerners into becoming just ordinary mainstream Americans. I suppose they didn't realize that it would make us Republicans. But, in fact, the South is Bush country just to the extent it has been de-Southernized. The great M.E. Bradford pointed out long ago that a "conservative" (*i.e.*, Republican) in the South is not the same thing as a Southern Conservative.

# The Yankee Problem

Some of the Blue fury against the Red states arises from the claim that the Blues pay more to the federals than they get back, that is, they are subsidizing us Red staters. I have always been skeptical of the claim that the South was a net economic gainer from the federal government. Are we to believe that Blues are so generous and benevolent that they are supporting us? To believe that is to deny three centuries of Yankee behaviour to the contrary and the evident nature of the liberal ruling class today. Raw state data about taxes paid and federal disbursements received tell us very little about who gets the profits. For instance, every time a Southern state institutes a new federally mandated program, Blue staters are imported to take all the high-paying jobs, and Blue state consultants and suppliers get a lot of the cash.

Of course, the Blues are not really serious about secession. Yankees have no civilization – only money and ideology. Without us to abuse and claim to feel superior to, they would not exist. Nevertheless, it is wonderful that the idea of secession – that is, self-government and devolution of power – has been given some public exposure. After all, our Founding Fathers affirmed that governments rest on the consent of the governed, who may alter or abolish them. If the United States was a normal country, the idea of breaking down a federal government that has grown much too big would be a normal part of political discourse. But, alas, the United States is not a normal country; it is the cannon fodder for a ruling class driven so mad by wealth and power that it seeks to dominate the Earth.

Reading the left wing anti-war commentary (as opposed to the conservative, *i.e.,* patriotic, anti-war commentary), one gets the impression that Bush's belligerent foreign policy can be blamed on his being a Texan and a Christian. Of course, a Skull and Bones carpetbagger does not make a Texan. As for the carnival tent religion Bush professes, it is sadly true that it is pretty widespread in the South today. But it is not the Southern tradition.

The identification of God with America and the United States with infallible righteousness is Yankee stuff through and through. It is exactly the type of "religion" that was used to deify Lincoln and justify the conquest of the South in 1861–1865. In Yankee history it is the stage they went through between the hyper-Calvinism of their early days and their present atheism. It did not arrive in Dixie until the early 20th century when various evangelists began imitating the style and content of the Yankee Billy Sunday. (See "The Real Old Time Religion" by the late theologian A.J. Conyers.) Traditional Southern clergymen would have made short shrift of heretical mountebanks like Pat Robertson.

The flourishing of Bushian religion, like the flourishing of the Republican Party, is a product of too many Southerners heeding the endless lectures about the need to forget the past, "join the 20th century," etc. The religion and the politics are the same thing, the adoption of discarded Yankee ideology that equates America with God.

Some Southerners are starting to show less of our traditional patriotic loyalty and more of the idiot nationalism that thinks the U.S. government and the President can do no wrong and are entitled to bomb anybody who disagrees. In both religion and politics, the dilution of Southern tradition has been a loss to Dixie – and to the whole country. For Southerners, and our sympathizers over the border, have always been the only true conservatives in the United States.

The country has continued its leftward roll for almost a half century now, despite repeated Republican election victories. Northern "conservatives," as the Rev. Robert Lewis Dabney pointed out 150 years ago, have never, in the entire course of American history, conserved anything. The leftward lurch corresponds exactly in time with the loss of power of the old-time Southern Democrats in Congress.

There have been grave mistakes in the course of Southern history, apart from the original one of going naïvely into a Union with bad people. There was Bragg commanding the Army of Tennessee and Longstreet fumbling at Gettysburg. In the same class is the decision of Southern leaders, when they were kicked out of the Democratic Party, to join the Republicans rather than form our own party. As a result, we are powerless. It was probably inevitable but nevertheless a great loss. Today there are no Southerners in Congress or in governors' chairs – only Republicans and Democrats.

But we still have something the Yankees don't have and have never had. There are still people writing books and poems and songs about Dixie. There is, despite all, a real Southern culture left. If you want to put secession on the table, let's consider the only part of the United States that really could be its own country. A true culture is the best basis for a viable country. Compared to that, all the Blue state talk of secession amounts to nothing but an adolescent tantrum at not having everything exactly their own way.

# Yankees vs. Yorkers: Cultural Cleansing, Phase One

*New England—where people get together to change the world!*
—Heard on PBS radio

IN 1833 JAMES FENIMORE COOPER returned from a European tour to Cooperstown — founded by his father, one of the first pioneers into the then still dangerous frontier of New York beyond the Hudson Valley. Cooper property included a pretty peninsula on Lake Otsego that the family had allowed the community to use for fishing, picnics, and boating. On arrival Cooper saw that the locals had appropriated the property to do with as they pleased. When he objected he found himself denounced by Whig newspapers throughout the region as a cruel, grasping aristocrat, an enemy of the people.

Along with his fellow Yorker Washington Irving, Cooper had already made a name for American letters. His novels created the archetypal Western hero, "The Deerslayer," and celebrated the patriotism and heroism of the War of Independence. For a decade after 1833 he abandoned adventure tales and became a novelist of manners.His theme was the overwhelming of the old New York culture by Yankees, the overflow of population from crowded and infertile New England. Cooper's region not only developed from wilderness to settled land during his lifetime, it underwent a demographic change that altered his state's society and culture. The old Anglo-Dutch society of the New York colony was unique but resembled the South more than New England. In the same period Cooper also produced *The American Democrat* as a complaint against the political and social trends that were replacing the republicanism of the Fathers. It was a direct product of his encounters with the Yankees on his home turf.

One must understand that prior to the War Between the States, "Yankee" was a particular ethnic designation. In fact, the very term may have arisen

18

among Hudson Valley Dutchmen to designate their disagreeable neighbours to the east. It was not the South but New England that was considered by most Americans to be the odd and "different" region, especially after its venomous Federalism and its treachery during the War of 1812. "Yankee" identified New Englanders as a distinct type at home or in the areas further west where they clustered. It was not a particularly complimentary designation, suggesting pushiness, religious hypocrisy, and sharp trading. Readers today miss the import of Irving's tale of "The Headless Horseman." It was about removing from New York the presumptuous Connecticut Yankee Ichabod Crane. Young Abe Lincoln out in Indiana and Illinois had a fund of "Yankee" stories to amuse the boys around the cracker barrel, although they were not as popular as his dirty stories.

Cooper spent his later years in the midst of the first big minority take-over in national history. There had previously been the displacement of the Indians, Massachusetts's purging of Baptists, Quakers, and witches, and the flight of the Tories, but nothing on the scale that overtook New York State in the early 19th century. By 1840 the majority of the population of New York State was New England born. In New York City the leading editors like William Cullen Bryant and Horace Greeley and the financiers were Yankees. Most rising state political leaders were of Yankee background.

Critics have tended to ignore or dismiss Cooper's books of this period as inferior or demonstrations of personal pique, but he was actually reflecting in literature an important phase of American history. *Homeward Bound* and *Home as Found* concern the Effingham family. The "LittlepageMss." (*Satanstoe, the Chain-Bearer,* and *The Redskins*) portray the family of that name and their friends and associates. The Effinghams and the Littlepages are traditional people. They live on the land. They deal generously with their neighbours and dependents. They enjoy the innocent pleasures of visiting, hunting, fishing, boating, ice skating, horse racing, and chaste courtship. They are sincere but tolerant Christians. They served in war against the Tories and Indians when called upon. They are full of good will and live-and-let-live. They have no agenda to impose and seek no power in government. They were the American form of the best of British civilisation and an example of what the Founders meant by communities of Liberty.

Returning to New York from Europe, the Effinghams must deal with the Yankee incomers Aristabulus Bragg and Steadfast Dodge, the latter name a beautiful invocation of the slippery character of the Yankee in operation. The theme is developed further and more subtly when the Littlepages face on home ground the also appropriately named Jason Newcome from Connecticut. The Yankees are contemptuous of good manners, boastful, ever ready to cast away traditions for the newest idea, and see making money as the chief object of life. Equality and majority rule for them should determine everything — in society and culture as well as before the law. Whatever "the people" want is theirs and whoever opposes is an evil enemy of the people, defending unfair privilege and oppressive traditions. They exemplify what Cooper was observing and deploring in *The American Democrat*. A major argument of that work is that "the people" did not mean majority rule but an amorphous, irresponsible, and manipulatable "public opinion" created by rogues — government rent-seekers, political party operatives, and shameless newspaper editors.

Democracy was no longer a matter of liberty under law but had become a matter of power and appetite. "Democracy" was coming to mean that people had a right to whatever they happened to want, the law and private rights be damned. Because power came from "the people," politicians were pretending that it had no limits and that their own self-serving interests were the will of the people. "He who would be a courtier under a king, is almost certain to be a demagogue in a democracy," Cooper wrote. In both cases, the ruler was being cleverly flattered for the benefit of the courtier.

"Jason Newcome" from Connecticut is portrayed in the Littlepage trilogy as the personification of the "democratic" revolution in New York society and politics:

Jason had a liberal supply of Puritanical notions, which, were bred in-and-in in his moral and, I had almost said, in his physical system...this man had strong points about him, and a native shrewdness that would have told much more in his favour had it not been accompanied by a certain evasiveness of manner, that caused one constantly to suspect his sincerity, and which often induced those who were accustomed to him to imagine he had a sneaking propensity that rendered him habitually hypocritical. Jason held New York in great contempt, a feeling he was not always disposed to conceal and of necessity his comparisons were usually made with the state of things in Connecticut, and much to the advantage of the latter.

However, Jason did admire the rising class of newly rich men in, New York City, "for he never failed to defer to money, come in what shape it would. It was the only source of human distinction he could clearly comprehend." Jason was certainly hard-working and enterprising. He managed to get control (often clandestinely) of many of the essential businesses of the community — the tavern, store, and lumber and grist mills — and to get whatever local office he wanted. Cooper vividly describes how the rising and astute politician Newcome pre-managed and packed a supposedly open citizens' meeting to give the imprimatur of "publick opinion" to his agenda. Jason, as Cooper character observes, "was a leading politician, a patriot by trade, and a remarkable and steady advocate of the rights of the people, even to minutiae. Those who know mankind will not be surprised…to hear it added that he was a remarkable rogue in the bargain."

A little thought and non-pious examination of American history will teach that Cooper was describing a prevailing aspect of our public life right up to the present day. H.L. Mencken, who was notoriously disdainful of Cooper's fiction, said that in *The American Democrat* Cooper was "the first American to write about Americans in a really fresh spirit" and that "his prophecies were as sound as his observations were accurate." Too true.

The Yankees' depredations upon society and manners were as bothersome to Cooper as their depredations upon politics and economy. They were pushy social climbers, insisting that their betters treat them as equals, but refusing to grant the same to those who were less successful and prosperous. Jason presumed an intimate friendship with mere acquaintances and "insisted to the last that he knew every gentleman in the county, whom he had been accustomed to hear alluded to in discourse." He was so officiously over-attentive to a lady, that she had to tell him in refusing his ministrations: "When I go to Connecticut, I shall feel infinitely indebted to you for another such offer."

The Yankees valued education and pioneered in public schools. But for Cooper and many others it was a superficial education that promoted presumptuousness while falling far short of the kind of learning needed for good leadership. It created a population able to read the newspapers but not wise enough to see through them. Cooper has fun telling how the Yankees changed the pioneer town name of Satanstoe, which was based on an unusual geographic feature, to the "respectable" Dibbleton.

One of Coopers characters, who has painfully observed the dubious methodology of Jason's rise to wealth and power, comments:

> I never could explain the process by means of which Jason wound his way into everybody's secrets.... The people of New England have a reputation this way...everything and everybody were brought under rigid church government among the Puritans; and when a whole community gets the notion that it is to sit in judgment on every act of one of its members, it is quite natural that it should extend that right into an enquiry into all his affairs. One thing is certain: our neighbours of Connecticut do assume a control over the acts and opinions of individuals that is not dreamed of in New York.

"A Yankee is never satisfied unless he is making changes," says one of Cooper's characters. "One half of his time, he is altering the pronunciation of his own names, and the other half he is altering ours." "I doubt if all this craving for change has not more of selfishness in it than either of expediency or philosophy," wrote Cooper, an insight that strikes a chord with conservatives of all times. The Connecticut newcomers, it seems, regarded themselves as more righteous and enlightened than the sinful New Yorkers among whom they settled, and therefore felt that they were entitled to change their ways and appropriate their property. It was a normal means of proceeding in their Puritan heritage for the Yankees to justify themselves by portraying those who opposed them as bad people with evil motives. "These men inevitably quarrel with all above them, and, with them, to quarrel is to calumniate." The "Chainbearer," a venerable surveyor as honest and benevolent as the day is long, finds that he has become known as "an old rogue" among people who have never even met him — slander spread because of his opposition to Jason's schemes. Over his self-serving agenda, the Yankee "throws a beautiful halo of morality and religion, never even prevaricating in the hottest discussion, unless with the unction of a saint."

Thus Cooper identified the historical origins of the perpetual crusades for the reform and reconstruction of society that diminish American liberty and independence.

The Yankee immigrants to New York State created the "the Burnt Over District," a phenomenon well-known to antebellum Americans. Western New York was thus labeled because it had been swept over by so many furious fires of evangelism, reform, and fanaticism. Anti-Masonry, Mormonism, prohibition, vegetarianism, Seventh Day Adventism, and socialist experiments all had their origins in the Burnt Over District. Then there was the first "women's rights" convention at Seneca Falls and the "free love" colony at Oneida. But progressively the great reformist cause became abolitionism, which had less to do with the welfare of African-Americans than it did with hatred of the South as an obstacle to Yankee economic projects and to Yankee dominion over the idea and the reality of America. The region became the base for John Brown's terrorism and generated vigilante mobs that discouraged independent thinkers.

Like most moderate Northerners, Cooper regarded agitation against slavery in the South as unconstitutional, unwise, and counter-productive. He agreed with John Adams that American slavery was mild and that slaves were no worse off than the lower class of Northern workers. He comments of slavery: "It is an evil, certainly, but in a comparative sense, not as great an evil as is usually imagined. There is scarcely a nation of Europe that does not possess institutions that inflict as gross personal privations and wrongs, as slavery." It is quite possible for a slaveholder to be a good Christian, Cooper wrote.

When Cooper wrote in *The American Democrat* that "the union of these States is founded on an express compromise, and it is not its intention to reach a benefit, however considerable, by extorting undue sacrifices from particular members of the confederacy," he doubtless had in mind the Whig "protective" tariff that exploited the South. And Cooper (as did Tocqueville and countless other non-Southerners) assumed it to be uncontested that the

Union was "a compact between separate communities," something that was later claimed to be an artificial and evil-minded Southern invention.

While the Yankee overflow was imposing its values on Old York State, the home country was at work on its own cultural cleansing. In the first American geography book, the author, Jedediah Morse of Connecticut, depicted New Englanders as an ideal people and most of the rest of Americans as shiftless barbarians. In his "American" dictionary, Noah Webster, also from Connecticut, announced that New Englanders spoke the best and purist English *in the world.* In his speller Webster introduced the peculiar spellings that supposedly differentiate us from Old England and which annoy the spellcheckers of those of us who try to write correct English.

At the same time New Englanders embarked on a deliberate campaign (and you can prove this chapter and verse) to seize control of American history. While the South was making history in the first half of the 19th century the Yankees were writing it and setting in stone the tale of the Revolution as a New England enterprise, ignoring or slighting the contributions of everybody else. They were so successful that even today most people are unaware of the important and decisive events of the Revolution carried on by Southerners in the South; and George Washington can be portrayed with a Northern accent and nobody notices.

A similar campaign was waged to establish New England literature as American literature. A host of self-promoting and mutually admiring scribblers pretty well managed to submerge the better antebellum American writers not of their ilk. As a result, generations of American schoolboys have been turned off literature forever by being force-fed the arrogant gurus Emerson and Thoreau and the jingles of Longfellow and Whittier as the best of American writing. Edgar Allan Poe hilariously punched holes in the Yankee pretensions in literature and William Gilmore Simms and others pointed out the lies in their history books. But once the South was crushed and impoverished there was no real opposition to New England dominion over letters and history.

For Cooper, the greedy rent-seekers through government and the moralistic reformers were but two sides of the same coin in the subverting of

American liberty: "The American doctrinaire is the converse of the American demagogue, and, in his way, is scarcely less injurious to the publick.... These opposing classes produce the effect of all counter-acting forces, resistance, and they provoke each others' excesses." Was he describing the sham battles between "liberals" and "conservatives" that make up most of American politics almost two centuries later? "Democracy" of this new sort had brought the politicization of social and moral life into campaigns for the alleged improvements that were necessary for "democracy" to be fulfilled. This was contrary to the individual liberty that Cooper believed the American founding had intended. It made "democracy" into a crusade rather than a legal framework of freedom — it was all about power rather than freedom.

Always the agenda to change Americans to fit the latest abstract pattern. Proposed as progress but actually a self-referential exercise of dominion by the elect. Education turned from creating good men and women to creating obedient tools — beginning with Horace Mann in 19th century Massachusetts and culminating with John Dewey (Vermont-born). Imperial wars against the South and the Filipinos and entrance into the carnage of the Great War glorified as righteous crusades. Fill in your own disfavoured imposition and you will find that it traces back one way or another to old New England, the Burnt Over District, or the upper Midwest and West Coast settled by Yankees.

A Vermont-born President declared that the business of American is business. A Connecticut-born President declared that the business of America is leading a New World Order. Another Connecticut-born President announced that the business of America is "global democracy" and at the same time urged us to meet a crisis by going shopping. For Cooper, the business of America was liberty. Or such it had been intended to be.

"The end of liberty is the happiness of man," wrote James Fenimore Cooper, "and its means, that of leaving the greatest possible personal freedom of action, that comports with the general good." Americans have "democracy," he added, but they are more under the rule of extra-legal authority than almost any people in the world. The all-important question was "whether principles are to rule this republic, or men; and these last, too, viewed in their most vulgar and repulsive qualities.It is time that the

American began to see things as they are, not as they are said to be, in the speeches of governors, Fourth of July orations, and electioneering addresses."

# The Yankee Way of War

WHY SHOULD ANYONE be surprised at the prisoner tortures carried on by the U.S. armed forces in Iraq? Given the low quality of our national leaders and the amoral atmosphere of the forces, only an imperviously smug belief in American exemption from human evil could blind anyone to the likelihood of such. In October 2001, early in the Afghan War and before the Iraq debacle had begun, in a piece called "Whom the Gods Would Destroy"* I pointed out that we were in the power of a bully of a Defense Secretary and a mentally and morally dysfunctional President, and that too many Americans were in an irresponsibly bellicose mood more indicative of thoughtless aggression than of the sober determination with which people ought to go about avenging a great wrong.

I quoted the warnings of Richard Weaver and Alesandr Solzhenitsyn on the descent into brutality that beckoned. The points made then seem to me a little prophetic and still valid. I would add that the American military has always swung back and forth between two modes or spirits. The Washington/Lee mode and the Grant/Sherman mode. The first emphasizes skill, enterprise, and courage in achieving objectives with an economy of force and strives to keep warfare as honourable as possible. The second relies on marshalling overwhelming materiel to crush a weak opponent, heedless of the cost in life and taxes, and rewards its commanders appropriately. The Grant/Sherman mode is self-righteous and recognizes no ends except boastful triumph. Our bureaucratized, politicized, technocratic armed forces have been in the amoral Grant/Sherman mode for a long time now. What kind of a regime sends women into harm's way and makes them into prison guards? Surely one not worth the allegiance of a civilized person.

---

*See *The Republicans: Annals of the Stupid Party* (forthcoming from Shotwell Publishing)

# The Enemy Up Close

A review of *The Beechers: An American Family in the Nineteenth Century*
by Milton Rugoff

---

AMERICAN PROTESTANTISM divides into two distinct cultural traditions dating back to colonial times. One tradition derives from New England and is Calvinist in origin; the other is Southern and Anglican. Anglican must be understood here as referring to a spirit rather than a structure, the structure having been largely dissolved by the American frontier.

This dichotomy has gone largely unnoticed for several reasons. For one thing, it does not follow denominational lines. Also, though the latter tradition may include more adherents, the former has had better publicity, greater prestige, and more get-up-and-go. Many Americans scarcely know that the second tradition exists and think that the first *is* American Protestantism. The New England tradition is Puritan, that is, disciplined, communal, and concerned with the "purification" of the community. It is parent to the American civil religion, a fact easily demonstrated by the allusions in Presidential addresses to America as "a city upon a hill."

The Southern tradition is largely folkish and focuses upon the individual and the state of his soul. It goes quietly about its work and is forbearing toward the mote in its neighbour's eye. Its evidences, being largely manifested in private life and often among people beneath the notice of intellectuals, are seldom recorded by either contemporary observers or historians. Because of the ignorance of the intellectuals, its presence and significance have been greatly underestimated in American history.

One can grasp the distinction between these two varieties of Protestantism by imagining two different churches on the same Sunday morning. One church is in Massachusetts, say, or Michigan. The preacher sermonizes on "World Peace" and the congregation sings "The Battle Hymn of the

Republic." The other church is in rural North Carolina, or perhaps Oklahoma, or a blue-collar section of Los Angeles. The sermon is on "Salvation" and the hymn is "In the Sweet Bye and Bye."

There is no question that the first church represents far more worldly power and prestige than the other, so much so that even late-comers to these shores often imitate it, unconsciously recognizing that assimilation to the New England model is the most respectable form of Americanization. One can find American nuns whose rhetoric and political activism resemble New England Unitarianism more closely than anything in European Catholicism. Martin Luther King, a man raised in the second tradition, became, almost instantaneously, a power in the land when he shrewdly resorted to New England-style rhetoric.

To distinguish these two traditions further, one need only consider two manifestations of the divergent traditions in human behaviour. As a demonstration of the Anglican tradition let's take General Lee, who reconciled the duties of a soldier with unostentatious faith and piety as successfully as is possible in an imperfect world, so successfully that he provided a model for millions of what used to be known as "Christian gentlemen." General Lee understood Christianity as an imperative struggle for personal virtue, its social relevance being that a virtuous man is always valuable to his fellows. For the contrasting example, one can find no better than Henry Ward Beecher, General Lee's contemporary and the most famous reforming preacher of his generation. Beecher understood the imperative of Christianity as one of social improvement, and personal virtue as consisting largely of being on the right political side.

Milton Rugoff's thorough and intimate history of three generations of Beechers is an admiring but candid account of a brilliant, energetic and forceful family. His treatment of the Beechers shows the transformation of American society in the 19th century from Puritanism to Victorianism. Rugoff's book also offers a close-up view of the first of the two Protestant traditions and of how it was transformed, by virtue of the Civil War, from a peculiarity of New England into the American tradition. The intellectual, spiritual, and public careers of the Beechers exemplify that merging of democracy and purification ritual that has provided the predominant tone of

American politics right down to the present. First there was Lyman Beecher, the leading Calvinist theologian of his day, who was instrumental in spreading the gospel to the West. (The "West" in New England parlance referred to areas north of the Ohio River settled by New Englanders. Nothing else counted.) Among Lyman's numerous children were Catherine Beecher, a pioneer feminist; Harriet Beecher Stowe, "the little woman who made the big war," in Lincoln's phrase; Henry Ward Beecher, the most admired and highest-paid preacher of his day; and a raft of other sons, all of them reformist clergymen.

This intimate review of the Beechers not only helps one understand the 19th century, but it has a more urgent pertinence as well. Let us assume that in the future some scholar will wish to write an objective history of the 1960s and 1970s in America. (It is optimistic, I know, to hope that anyone will survive our educational debacle and declining opportunities for free speech with sufficient intellectual curiosity and ability.) The most difficult problem such a historian will face in understanding these two decades will be this: How did it happen that during that epoch such a large number of people with low ethical and moral standards and transparently self-interested and destructive motives managed to pass themselves off as the moral leaders and benefactors of society?

This question can be answered only by looking back to the reformist movements of the 19th century and to the precedents and parallels they provided for our more recent ravaging of order and decency in the name of moral vision. The 1960s and 1970s resemble no period in American history so much as the 1850s. The keynote of both eras is irresponsible destruction and aggression in the name of democratic fulfillment. The earlier crusade, though now long hallowed by success, can be seen, when viewed through the medium of the Beechers, to have been as ambiguous in motivation and results as the later one.

The closest resemblance of the two periods is in the presence of that now familiar intolerance and the extravagance of rhetoric and action that kicks over the traces of normal political life and postulates goals so self-evidently righteous that disagreement is *sin,* explicable only as the work of the devil. This style of politics demonizes the opposition and deifies itself. Anyone who has observed politics in this country in recent decades understands the extent to which such violent and antirational posing has held sway in public discourse. The 1850s supply the model. From the imposing authority of his pulpit, Henry Ward Beecher exhorted young men to depart for Kansas and kill Southern settlers. This rhetoric represented more than the momentary and overwrought emotions of one man: it reflected the behaviour of a large number of people and spilled over into private, apolitical matters.

When Harriet visited the South for the first time — after the War — she was quite astounded to encounter families who were kindly, cultivated, Christian, *and* militant rebels. Rugoff comments: "She had seen the barbarous enemy the face of evil and found that his sins had left no mark on him." But the Puritan ritual of demonization had already done its work. It is not the Beechers' desire for social improvement that should trouble us, but the self-aggrandizement and disregard for consequences with which it was pursued. From the phenomenon of busing, as with other social issues, we, too, have grown familiar with absentee moralism. Henry did all he could to hasten the onset of the conflict, but during the War which he had helped to produce and in which over 600,000 men died, the famous clergyman lived in luxury in Newport and Europe.

Recall also the 1970s, when philosophical and psychological weirdness sprouted constantly from the same soil as liberal politics. Again the parallels and precedents are evident. The Beechers were almost all involved in spiritualism. Professor Stowe, Harriet's husband, had frequent "visions." Harriet, in response to the remark that the creator of Uncle Tom had never been to the South, said: "No, but it all came to me in visions, one after another, and I put them down in words." "There is no arguing with pictures," she explained on another occasion, a sentiment that would doubtless please our electronic journalists. One does not have to be a latter-day defender of slavery to recognize the disastrous consequences that ensued when people like the Beechers took slavery out of the arena of political realities in which the Founding Fathers had dealt with it and placed it in the realm of fiction, propaganda, sentimentality, and emotional self-indulgence.

By now we are all familiar with the extent to which the Great Society and its various attendant crusades for justice provided a cover for private pocket lining. One recalls various political figures who were simultaneously great civil rights advocates and outright crooks. There seems an inescapable affinity between a certain kind of politically mobilized morality and dishonesty. Both Henry and Harriet became wealthy because of their antislavery positions. Harriet purchased a confiscated Florida plantation for a pittance. Henry's favourite money-maker was a mock slave auction that he staged over and over again. On every occasion the "slave" was young, attractive, female and almost white; there is no recorded instance of an "auction" of a male, child, or ugly female "slave."

To draw a close to our catalogue of precedents, there is a high correlation in both the 1850s and our own era between reformist politics of the Puritan stripe and sexual promiscuity and opportunism. We all know now that the New Frontier-Great Society epoch was marked by a cynical jettisoning of tradition al sexual morality by the occupants of the seats of power, and that much of the elan that fueled the New Left in the streets, and still fuels its fellow travelers in positions of power, resulted from the euphoria of the early stages of sexual license. The rhetoric, however, was mostly about peace and justice.

Henry Ward Beecher, the most popular preacher in America, famous for his spellbinding crusades against slavery, liquor, the secret vice, and every other evil, committed adultery with at least one woman of his congregation, a woman who happened also to be a Sunday School teacher and the wife of an admiring protégé of Beecher's. The offense itself is not so revealing as the spirit of callous exploitation with which it was carried out and the deceit and hypocrisy with which it was covered up. Beecher was warmly defended by the establishment of his day. Most of the press declared his innocence and his parishioners raised $100,000 for his legal expenses, while those who brought the charges that we now know to be true were hounded. The powers that be, then as now, rush to the rescue when their most valuable asset, their pretense of superior moral vision, is threatened. Henry's deceit in this episode was not merely a weakness displayed on one painful occasion. It was a way of life to a man whose fame and riches were built upon a conveniently abstract, unscrupulously aggressive, politically irresponsible moralizing. In his memoirs, for example, Henry lied about so simple a thing as a college debate. He recounted an occasion in which he had carried the house against a proposal for the colonization of blacks outside the United States. In fact, he had not participated in the debate in question and the pro-colonization side had won. Characteristically, he had falsely glorified his own role and distorted the historical record to make his antislavery stand date to a much earlier and more dangerous period than it actually did.

The story of the Beechers is that of people who proclaimed themselves the champions of freedom and morality and demonized those who disagreed, while all the time keeping their hand in the till and their eye on the main chance. The chief lesson we can learn is that there is something in the American fabric that guarantees that now and then such people will succeed outrageously. Today's secular liberals will, of course, dismiss Henry Ward Beecher as simply a typical hypocritical Protestant moralist. Yet he was one of them. He was a leading liberal of his day, a crusader not for *souls* but for political and social reform. He was an establishment figure, not a small-town vigilante. He spoke from a position of power and respectability from which he safely and irresponsibly rode to the outer limits every fad of his day. Beecher is not the father of the Moral Majority; he is the father of the smug establishment figures who juggle morality and sybaritic life-styles in an everlasting shell game. Today's morality movement comes out of that other, quieter, Protestant tradition. Its adherents are the attacked, not the attackers. They are not dogmatists seeking to impose their narrow standards on more enlightened fellow citizens. They are rather provoked into defending their communities and standards from impositions by the arrogant purveyors of a false and imperialistic ethos.

That strange combination of Puritanism and democracy that wreaked so much havoc in the 19th century, having done its work and reached the natural limits of its expansion, began a retreat into narrower and less dangerous limits after the debacle of Reconstruction. Something very similar is perhaps happening now. If so, we can hope once again for leaders for whom public life, as for Lee, is an arena for the exercise of private virtue rather than, as for the Beechers, a vehicle for the social mobilization of private greed and discontent.

# The Flight of the Kiwis

A review of *Descent from Glory: Four Generations of the John Adams Family*
by Paul C. Nagel

---

JOHN ADAMS was descendedfrom a long line of Puritan yeomanry who were among the earliest settlers of Massachusetts. Though his father never achieved anything more than a modest local distinction, John Adams became a key figure in the Revolution in New England, leading member of the First and Second Continental Congresses, political philosopher, diplomat, Vice-President, and President. But his greatest accomplishment was his marriage to Abigail Smith, one of the most remarkable women in American history, who added Anglican gentry, including the distinguished Quincy line, to the family stock. Of the four children of this remarkable couple who reached maturity, only one achieved distinction. John Quincy Adams recapitulated his father's success as a scholar, diplomat, Secretary of State, and President. But John Quincy's two brothers, Charles and Thomas Boylston, died young from alcoholism. His sister, Abigail, married William Stephens Smith, one of the most irresponsible and unscrupulous promoters of the day. Smith had all of Aaron Burr's profligacy and ambition, without Burr's charm and courage. He died owing vast sums and left his family destitute.

John Quincy Adams repeated the family pattern in more than his successes. His marriage was the luckiest aspect of his career. His wife was Louisa Johnson, daughter of a Southern family and the most attractive of all the Adamses. Louisa shrunk under the puritanical conceit and censoriousness of her husband, which was directed at himself, his family, and the world, but she never completely withered away. Though she wasn't to achieve the exemplary republican matronliness of Abigail, her kindness and liveliness were responsible for whatever was attractive in the later generations of Adamses. As is usually the case, the women made up the better part of the family.

Of the three sons of John Quincy and Louisa, John, Jr. died young after failing miserably in business and George Washington was a suicide before age 30, after what was referred to in the 19th century as a career of debauchery.

Again, one son redeemed the line. Charles Francis vindicated the high opinion the Adamses held of themselves by his achievements as a congressman and scholar and as the chief architect of Northern diplomatic success in Europe during the Civil War. Of his seven children, four sons are noteworthy: the historians Henry and Brooks; John Quincy, a gentleman farmer who felt only weakly and intermittently the impulse to thrust himself before the public; and Charles Francis, Jr., the only one of the family who saw military service in the Civil War or who took any active part in the post-war building of the American economy.

Paul C. Nagel, in *Descent from Glory,* presents the sad story of the Adams family as a family, from the inside. He narrates with clarity and shows a deft mastery of the immense Adams documentation, certainly the largest of any American family (though, despite the vastness of the record, there are strategic lacunae in regard to each of the black sheep). He approaches the subject in a spirit of sympathetic candour rather than of muckraking, and he significantly adds to our awareness of the 19th century America that lay beneath political rhetoric.

What strikes us most deeply in this sad account is the old, old lesson of the vanity of human ambition and the inevitable doom of all dreams of dynasty-building in a republic. What a price the Adamses paid for the ambition that flowed only too naturally from their talents and for those secularized remnants of their Calvinist conscience which left them, in the final analysis, unable to love themselves and even unable to love Creation except on their own unattainable terms! How much happier they would have been had they been able to confine themselves to the family circle and devote their talents to practical, local beneficence or to the vindication of American intellect!

In this admirable study, Nagel does not seek to draw sweeping lessons. He is content to show how the warring devils of ambition and conscience wreaked havoc time and again on those members of the family who were unable or unwilling to adapt to so relentless a view of life. A Puritan conscience can only avoid disaster if it is chastened by practical application or when it is balanced, as it was in the Founders and in the best of English statesmen, by a Cavalier magnanimity and sense of proportion.

Taking the Adamses as exemplary of the New England "aristocracy," history affords few examples of so swift and uncontested a decline. For the first half of the 19th century the heirs of New England and Southern Founders engaged in mortal combat to control the destiny of America. New Englanders devoted themselves with Puritan zeal to the destruction of the Cavalier side of the English inheritance, the Southern gentry, and the annihilation of whom was to them the sine qua non of national progress. When the contest was over, New England had an immense share of the political and economic power of America and a near-total monopoly of the cultural power. Yet the fourth generation of Adamses, despite all their advantages and responsibilities, fastidiously picked up their skirts and retired to carp that things had not turned out as they expected. Henry and Brooks spent their talents blaming their own and their country's degradation on Southerners, Jews, the predetermined forces of history, uncouth new men like Grant (who were but the natural outcome of their own vision) — on everything except themselves. By contrast, the Southerners staked all on their vision, lost, and retired from the field chastened but with their honour intact.

The self-emasculation of the Adamses in the fourth generation was the real descent from glory. New England fell swiftly from overwhelming predominance into genteel irrelevance or arrogant nullity. To the extent that the Puritan ideal of America was preserved, it was preserved by simple, clearheaded Midwesterners, sprung of common or immigrant stock, who went to work to redeem the American dream and to preserve the American sense of decency. To the extent that that decency was preserved, it was largely extra-political. Politics was accepted as a degraded sphere, tolerable only because it was unimportant. The great dream of republican ethics and virtue that had inspired the Founders was dead, never to be resurrected. This descent from glory was more than the tragedy of one family. It was an American tragedy, the echoes of which still reverberate down the long hall of history.

# Origins of the Educational Nightmare

Review of *Destroying the Republic: Jabez Curry and the Re-education of the Old South* by John Chodes

JABEZ LAMAR MONROE CURRY of Alabama (1825—1903) was one of those fairly numerous 19th century Americans whose lives of astounding talent and energy put to shame the diminished leaders of the U.S. in the 21st century. Or rather would put them to shame if they had sufficient intelligence to distinguish their own inferior quality.

Learned and articulate, a lawyer, Baptist minister, college president, diplomat, member of the U.S. and Confederate congresses, Confederate combat officer, prolific and eloquent writer and orator, Curry was a significant public figure from the 1850s to the 1890s. (Put beside Curry or any of his contemporary peers, George W. Bush and Teddy Kennedy look like dull-witted adolescents.)

Mr. Chodes's libertarian work on Curry's career is a rich source of understanding of many aspects of 19th century American history. Having the good fortune not to be a "professional historian," the author is able to see many things that the professionals have been socialized not to see. Fine as Mr. Chodes's work is, however, it leaves me with a serious unanswered question. Shall I put it on the shelf with the DiLorenzo School of revisionist Civil War history? Or with works on the evils of Reconstruction? Or beside John Taylor Gatto's *Underground History of American Education*?

The chapter on "Reconstruction as Re-Education" is alone worth the price of the book. The Marxist class conflict perspective, with a Gramscian twist, is now "mainstream" American history. All of American history has been distorted but no part more so than Reconstruction. Chodes shows that Reconstruction was more than a horror of military domination and economic exploitation. It was also a program of ideological and ethnic cleansing which continues to damage the American people in our own time.

The many observers who seem to think that militarism and abuse of citizens is an innovation of the Bush administration have evidently not familiarized themselves with President Grant and the Reconstruction Congress.

Those who think that federal control of education was an invention of the Democrats and the Great Society have a lot to learn. It was the Republican President Hayes who declared education to be one of "the rights of man" to be supported by taxation and devoted to inculcating national unity. His successor, the Republican Garfield, devoted his first message to Congress to promotion of federal funding of public schools. "It is the voice of the children of the land," declaimed Garfield, "asking us to give them all the blessings of our civilization."

Legislation to answer the voice of the children was pushed in Congress by New England Republicans in 1882—83 and barely failed of passage. This was seven years after the formal end of Reconstruction. The strongest public rationale, but not the only motive, was to alleviate the illiteracy of the freed people of the South. This rationale, like that of all the Reconstruction measures, was based on calculated misrepresentation of conditions in the South. Great strides were being made in education in the Southern states, which were devoting more of their resources to the effort, in proportion to their wealth, than Northern states (as they have ever since). Even greater progress would have been made if the funds Southerners had appropriated out of their poverty in the first years after the war had not been systematically stolen by the same Republicans who decried the South's ignorance. The National Bureau of Education, which from the 1880s was the chief instrument for carrotting and sticking American public schools into conformity with elitist plans, originated lock, stock, barrel, and personnel out of the Reconstruction Freedmen's Bureau which had been to a large extent the irresponsible and coercive de facto government of the South.

The Republican proponents of federal education were clear about their desire to create a system on the statist, militarized models of Europe. No

American educational ideas that preceded Horace Mann's Prussian/Massachusetts school system were to be considered. Black voters had to be subsidized enough to vote Republican and to be content where they were, else they might migrate to the North and West. They had to be kept in the South, which was the main theme of Northern politics throughout the 19th century, an even stronger imperative than the desire to loot the productive Southern economy. Further, federally-controlled, "free," universal, compulsory public schools were needed to control the immigrant masses of the northeast.

Behind it all, as Chodes shows, was a commanding assumption and necessity. As one New England promoter of federal education put it, "But for ignorance among the nominally free, there would have been no rebellion." If Southerners had not been too ignorant to understand the benefits of patterning themselves after New Englanders, there would have been no bloody war. To prevent decentralization in the future, Southern whites had to be cleansed of their "ignorance," that is, of their un-New England thoughts. Federal public schooling was also needed to confront the "hordes coming from beyond the great oceans." It had nothing to do with learning and everything to do with control of the population by their betters.

While the Republican plan for centralized and regimented public schools failed in the House of Representatives and had to wait some years before full implementation, all was not lost. The Morrill Act of the Lincoln administration took a long step toward federalizing higher education. (Senator Morrill of Vermont also gave his name to the biggest tariff in American history.) The Lincolnian Department of Agriculture was able to work itself into the public schools by "extension" agents. The philosophy of education that governed the department, as Chodes conclusively shows, was behaviourist, fully anticipating the psychological manipulation of children by the self-appointed wise and good that was the essence of Deweyism and is now entrenched national policy. Again, the barely vanquished Southern demon spurred on the effort. Southern devotion to such immaterial, reactionary ideals as courage and honour had been responsible for rebellion. Future generations must be made into pragmatic American materialists suitable for labour and production.

If the elite wise and good could not get sweeping federal legislation to further the control and conformity of education, they had another string to their bow. This is where the sad paradox of Jabez Curry comes in. This eloquent and indefatigable defender of the South and of the constitutional principles of the old republic spent the last two decades of his long life as head of the Peabody Educational Fund, a northern charity with several millions of dollars to be devoted to the advancement of education in the South. The work of Curry and the other elitists who controlled the great instruments of charitable wealth was devoted entirely to fostering a certain kind of education — universal, compulsory, "free," tax-supported graded public schooling. Besides relentless propaganda, their chief tool was the "matching" grant. Substantial amounts of cash were available to local and state authorities who would match the gifts out of tax-paid funds.

Thus were established, step by step, universal, compulsory state school systems, whose content and direction were essentially provided by Deweyite "normal schools." It should be noted that indirect control of public policy by institutions of great wealth (accumulated before the income tax) is now a norm of American government. Such leveraging of wealth into elitist political dictation is unconstitutional and undemocratic, but the Rockefeller, Carnegie, Ford, etc. foundations dictated much of the domestic social legislation and foreign policy of the United States in the 20th century. Their power is nearly as great as and even more irresponsible than that of the Supreme Court or the media. And it is never mentioned. George Wallace is the only public figure, to my knowledge, has ever called attention to this unelected power over the people of the United States.

The governing board of the Peabody endowment, supposedly a private charity, met in the White House and also counted the sitting President as a member. The nature of the whole enterprise is perhaps revealed in the fact that Grant, though a civilian, attended the meetings in full military regalia. Part of Peabody's fortune had been accumulated through the manipulation of fraudulent bonds of Southern carpetbagger state legislatures. J.P. Morgan was the manager of the trust. How did the ex-Confederate Curry become an instrument for the undoing of his own principles and his own people? For doing the bidding of rich inveterate South-haters? It was not simply a case of a defeated Confederate making the best of a bad situation. Education is, of course, a good thing. The South was poor and needed money for education. But why did a man like Curry buy the whole hog — not just education but universal, compulsory, "free," tax-supported schooling on a model dictated by the relentless Bostonian enemies of his blood?

Other articulate Southerners saw what was going on. Possibly Curry.

Curry saw it also but refused to acknowledge the truth. John Chodes shows us in revealing context and detail what happened. Why is perhaps one of those mysteries buried deep in the human heart.

It has long been an accepted article of faith among Americans that education is a good thing. That, indeed, it is a necessity for a free and self-governing people. But when and by whom was it determined that this desirable thing was to be universal, compulsory in attendance and tax support, "free," and devoted to inculcating government-coerced conformity? *Destroying the Republic* provides much of the answer to this vital question.

# "Tiger's Meat": William Gilmore Simms and the Yankee Distortion of Revolutionary History

WILLIAM GILMORE SIMMS, novelist, historian, poet, essayist, critic, editor, was the greatest Southern man of letters after the death of Edgar Allan Poe in 1849. He stood then, and stands now, much higher among American writers than has been acknowledged since the War Between the States.

Simms was also among the foremost authorities on the American War of Independence of his day. He had a large collection of original manuscripts (destroyed during Sherman's famous march through South Carolina) and had interviewed many surviving participants and their close relatives. He wrote a well-researched series of novels on the Revolution as well as what is still the best biography of Francis Marion. In the various journals which he edited and contributed to, Simms reviewed everything that appeared in print on the era (including a just but gentle treatment of Parson Weems's famous mythmaking about George Washington).

Unsurprisingly, Simms was in 1856 invited to lecture across New York State on the Chautauqua circuit on the subject of the Revolution in South Carolina. Not long into his tour he found himself greeted by so much orchestrated, prearranged personal and press hostility that he canceled. Simms had many friends and admirers among moderate Northerners. Although he had had some controversies with New England historians and critics, he was surprised by the extent to which South-hating frenzy had seized the Northern public in the Yankee-settled regions.

Reflecting at home on this experience, he wrote out three lectures that were delivered in South Carolina. These have remained in manuscript and have never been printed. In these lectures, entitled "South Carolina in the

Revolution: The Social Moral," Simms expressed an understanding of how the ground had been cut from under the shared national sentiment which he had done so much to cultivate. In "The Social Moral" Simms also shows his powers as a social observer in analysing the forces in Northern society that had destroyed fraternity, and also his powers as a historian in understanding the nature of the distortions, many still current today, that had been inflicted on the understanding of American history. [1]

Simms poses the rhetorical question, referring to the North: "Shall a whole people be fed, for near half a century upon tiger's meat, seasoned with viper's venom, nor raven like the one, nor sting fatally like the other!" Americans had once worked together for their liberty. The Union involved reciprocal bonds and courtesies and affections and compromises. What Simms discovered, and recorded with his usual penetration in "The Social Moral," was that the comity now only worked one way. Slurs against South Carolina's role in the Revolution were not misunderstandings. They were falsehoods with malice aforethought. They revealed beyond doubting the evil disposition of erstwhile compatriots.

In the early days of the United States, Founding Father Alexander Hamilton remarked: "The safety of a republic depends essentially on the energy of a common national sentiment." The common national sentiment of the antebellum years — among American peoples diverse in economic interests, folkways, and political agendas — mainly rested on a fraternal sense of the shared perils and triumphs of the War of Independence, which all Americans recognized as a revered founding. In the antebellum years most decent Americans shared in and gloried in this fraternal sense, as did Simms. All of Simms writing had been in the fraternal American spirit until he was forced to respond to an aggressive New England chauvinism which reinterpreted the Revolutionary experience as part of a highly partisan cultural agenda.

One of the pieties enforced since Appomattox is that Northern is national and Southern is, by definition and unexamined assumption, evilly-motivated "sectionalism." Thus Simms's concern for justice to South Carolina's role in the War of Independence in his response to unscrupulous and dishonest attacks is conventionally ascribed to a perverse "sectionalism."

A biographer plays to this assumption when he writes: "Simms, who was upset over the attacks by the Northern Congressmen and abolitionists regarding South Carolina's role in the Revolution, wanted to make his state proud of its past." To the contrary, Simms did not accuse South Carolinians of lack of pride but of lack of sufficient attention to substantiating their past. He informed his South Carolina audience: "But secure in our invincible self-esteem, — our chinese wall — which shuts us in, equally from the Barbarians, and ourselves, we never troubled ourselves on the subject of our real reputation, or the duties which it entailed upon us."

Simms had been celebrating the South Carolina Revolutionary experience as a contribution to the national sentiment that held the Union together from the earliest days of his career. And it is interesting, in regard to Simms's supposed "sectionalism," that in his foreword to the "new and revised" 1860 edition of his history of South Carolina, he makes not a single sectional remark, such as was commonplace with Northern writers, but instead indulges in civic piety and brilliant remarks about the purposes of history. [2]

On the other side, the New England campaign to get all the credit for the Revolution, like their campaign to use the Union for economic profit, had been going on almost from the beginning. In his autobiography Jefferson points out an instance, personally known to him, where Federalist historians had given Massachusetts credit for something that had been due to the action of Virginia. In the House of Representatives in 1798, Northern members were pushing for the funding of a regular army (an increase of centralized power) on the grounds that it was needed to defend the allegedly enervated South. Nathaniel Macon of North Carolina, who had fought through the Southern campaigns of the Revolution, remarked: "In the last war no man eastward of the Delaware was ever seen fighting in the Southern States, and that now the Southern members are satisfied, with few exceptions, to be left to themselves." [3]

Simms's attention to the question was first drawn by a work by one Lorenzo Sabine of Maine published in 1847: *American Loyalists, or Biographical Sketches of Adherents to the British Crown in the War of the Revolution: Alphabetically Arranged; with a Preliminary Historical Essay.* Sabine's work on American Loyalists is a very poor piece of scholarship, mostly a list of Tories. The historical essay that precedes the list, containing the claim that New Englanders had won the Revolution in the South while South Carolina had been "imbecile," is completely gratuitous and irrelevant to the subject of the book, as well as conspicuously false. Sabine, it may be noted, came from an area of Maine inhabited largely by Tories, but he makes no reference to personal experience. It was also an area notorious for trading with the enemy during the War of 1812.

Sabine claimed that South Carolina had been mostly Tory and so weak that the Revolution had been won in the South by soldiers from "the North." Sabine's attack on South Carolina's role in the Revolution was not a historiographical or literary fluke. It was a commonplace of New England discourse for a half-century previously. Such rhetoric was a function of the New England drive for hegemony that characterized the antebellum era.[4]

It is not possible to deal here with all of Sabine's falsehoods about the Revolution in the South. Simms did it very well. Some of Sabine's claims are simply silly. He asserts that South Carolinians were so enervated by slavery they were unable to defend Charleston. But New York, Boston, and Philadelphia had been occupied during much of the war, even though they were defended by the common army of the States! Charleston fell after a heroic resistance, surrendered by the Yankee general sent by the Continental Congress.

In his *Life of Francis Marion* (New York: George F. Coolidge & Brother, 1844), p. 306, Simms recounts events in the latter part of the war: "The armies led by Gates and Greene to the defense of Carolina, were truly from States north of her, but they were not the Northern States. Two fine bodies of troops came from Maryland and Delaware, but the rest were from Virginia and North Carolina — with the exception of the Pennsylvania Line which harbored mutineers and traitors." In fact, while many Southern volunteers served in the northern campaigns, no New England unit *ever* served in the South. (Unless one counts Connecticut and New York Loyalist regiments that fought on the British side.) Simms's articles on "The Revolution in South Carolina," in addition to being a mine of information, are a complete and true answer to all the aspersions and claims orchestrated by the New Englanders.

Contrary to the New England theoretical assertion, slavery did not weaken the South in war but was a source of strength, as the War of Southern Independence would later prove. But the biggest part of the lie rested on the numbers of troops in the Continental Line, in which New England was indeed overrepresented. The catch is that most of these troops were organized after the war had moved southward and saw little active service. They contributed little to the final victory in the Revolution which, as Macon pointed out and Simms substantiated, was won in the South by the partisans and Continental troops and militia from Delaware southward. Simms's essays on "The Revolution in South Carolina," in addition to being a mine of information, are a complete and true answer to all the aspersions and claims orchestrated by the New Englanders.[5]

In context it is well to remember that New England was held in disdain by many Americans because of traitorous activities during the War of 1812, something that was in the realm of common knowledge. Massachusetts, in a glaring assertion of state's rights, had withheld its militia from federal service during a time of invasion — and then for years had notoriously demanded from Congress compensation for its militia expenses. Unlike Southerners, the powers of New England had been indifferent or hostile to the vindication of national honour in the War of 1812 because they were making too much money in trade with wartime Europe to care.

The historian Harlow Sheidley describes how the leaders of Massachusetts sorely felt their declining national power after the War of 1812 and mounted a multifaceted campaign to regain what they regarded as their rightful pre-eminence. In a chapter called "Sectional Nationalism: Massachusetts Conservatives Interpret the American Past," she relates how her subjects moved to take over the history of the American Revolution and the definition of American nationalism. Daniel Webster's oration in Charleston, in which he celebrated the non-existent graves of New England Revolutionary soldiers in the South, seen in context, is merely a move in this campaign. Sheidley writes: a "properly constructed history" would promote the New England version of civic humanism and the political/economic agenda of nationalism. "Finally, the specific nature of the nationalism promoted by the Massachusetts conservatives' version of American history would advance their sectionalist claims" to national pre-eminence, would establish the centrality of

New England in American history, and "vindicate the claims of the state in producing the Revolution," thereby placing Massachusetts "in a position to which she is entitled."[6]

Sabine's account of South Carolina and New England in the American Revolution is nothing more nor less than a move in this game.

Not only Southerners were offended by the New England effort to claim all the glory of the Revolution. Pennsylvania writer Job R. Tyson wrote that "New Englanders had seized control of American history," claiming "the exclusive honour of having originated the free principles which followed our independence. They had garnered for their section the moral triumphs of the whole proud enterprise." If it were not countered, New England-centered history would pass to future generations as the accepted truth.[7]

Invited to lecture on the Revolution in New York In 1856, Simms had entered the belly of the beast. Western New York was not only the core of the Chautauqua circuit: Chautauqua was the name of a town in the region. It was also "the Burnt Over District," well-known in American popular lore as a hotbed of religious and social ferment. At the time of the Revolution western New York had been empty frontier. In the antebellum period it filled up with the overflow of the poorer population of New England. By 1830 half the people in New York State were New England-born and there was a very different social climate from that of Old Yorkers like James Fenimore Cooper, Washington Irving, James K. Paulding, or Mrs. Elizabeth F. Ellet, who wrote good non-sectionalist Revolutionary history that Simms admired. And in New York City, most of the big money men, and the leading editors like Bryant and Horace Greeley, were also Yankees.

The Burnt Over District was so called because it had been swept time and again by raging fires of evangelism and reform. The evangelism was post-millennial, a heretical form of Protestantism postulating the need to perfect man on earth before Judgment Day. At various times reform had focused on perfection of man by elimination of liquor, of tobacco, of meat-eating, of marriage, or other evils. When Simms in 1856 bearded the tiger, fervour had concentrated on the greatest evil in American society, the Southern slaveholder. America was God's instrument and God's Kingdom on earth, held back from perfection only by Southern wickedness.

If we draw the line of Simms's intended course from New York City to Buffalo in 1856, we will pass within a few miles of the center of the anti-Masonic paranoia of a few decades earlier; the place where Joseph Smith received the golden tablets of Mormon from the Angel Moroni; where William Miller began the Seventh Day Adventists by predicting, inaccurately, the date of the end of the world; the free love colony of John Humphrey Noyes at Oneida; the first feminist convention at Seneca Falls; and the area where John Brown lived and collected followers and financial backers.

Simms could not have picked a worse place to carry his temperate plea for fraternal sentiment in the history and credit of the Revolution. The area was awash with class and ethnic conflict, religious hysteria, and political paranoia. Once he had seen it first-hand, Simms described it well in "The Social Moral." Because of the ambitions and internal conflicts of the North, tensions had been diverted to an outside enemy, the South. The grounds of fraternal sentiment no longer held. The North no longer stood for what Simms described in "The Social Moral" as "harmony, union, and justice."

There was, but not alone, the Brooks-Sumner affair. Republicans were told by their newspapers and orators of a brutal attack by a Southern bully. They knew nothing of the provocation. They had been told of Bleeding Kansas, which, in accordance with Charles Sumner's speech, was all the fault of brutish Southerners. They knew little of Beecher's Bibles and of John Brown's mass murders.

The people of the Burnt Over District had long known that Southerners were alien and contemptible, inferior but dangerous. They now "knew" that Southerners were engaged in an evil conspiracy to dominate the Union, to spread slavery, to threaten and thwart everything good and decent valued by Northerners, like protective tariffs, internal improvements, and government-sponsored banking. Political tiger's meat indeed, thrown out for the advantage of the Republican agenda.

The hateful reaction that led Simms to cancel his lecture tour after a few outings was no isolated incident, nor was it a spontaneous outrage at the Brooks-Sumner affair. "Shall a whole people be fed, for near half a century upon tiger's meat, seasoned with viper's venom, not raven like the one, nor sting fatally like the other!" There was an election campaign going on in which the Republicans were highly organized for the first time. Hatred of the South had been whipped up by politicians and the yellow press. Mob intimidation of Democratic voters was not uncommon in the area. (See Harold Frederic's novel *The Copperhead*, which is exactly about this.)

In 1856, when Simms entered the Burnt Over District, the Republican Party had for the first time effectively combined the economic and cultural agendas of the dominant Northern class into an effective political movement, the lever of which was paranoia over the alleged Southern plot to spread slavery to the North.

In writing history Simms wanted to celebrate the republican United States and promote civic virtue. The purpose of the New Englanders was quite different: power. Simms was well aware of this and he was well aware, as was everyone at the time, of the very revealing pension question. Though they had received cash bonuses and large land bounties for their service, New Englanders were the main beneficiaries and promoters of the pension system established in the early 1800s. Pensions were at first thought of as being for disabled and impoverished veterans. By stages they were extended to all veterans and to their dependents and survivors. In 1830 there were more people on the pension rolls than had ever been in the Revolutionary army— the first great entitlement program.

Pensions were one of the biggest items in the federal budget and most of it went to New Englanders, some of whom had had only brief desultory service, while many of Marion's men could not document their much more hazardous and valuable services, or refused reward for their exercises of republican virtue. Southerners like Washington, John Taylor, and Nathaniel Macon had declined any financial rewards for their patriotic service.

Marcus Norton, a Democrat, one of the few truly national-minded governors of Massachusetts after the Revolution, writes to Secretary of War John C. Calhoun on May 6, 1818:

> But a sense of duty to my Country and its Government constrains me to make known to you some of the abuses of the Law for the relief of some of the soldiers of the Revolutionary Army, which are attempted to be practised and which, I trust you have the power to prevent. I learn, since my return to Massachusetts, that the applications for pensions under this law, are numerous beyond the expectations of any one: and that there are among the Applicants a very great number, who do not come within the literal or equitable provisions of the Act.

> I have no doubt that the officers of your department will exercise due vigilance (and no small share will be necessary) in preventing Militia and State troops from placing themselves upon the Continental Establishment.

> The great abuses to which I wish to call your attention, consist in the applications of men who are not in need of assistance from their Country for a support. Your directions allowing this fact to be proved by the oath of the applicant while it promotes and encourages perjury and gives the knave an advantage over the honest man, do not in any considerable degree check the abuses of which I complain. A great many in comfortable and easy and some in affluent circumstances, have already taken the oaths preparatory to their applications to your Department.[8]

When we think of Simms as an historian and "sectionalist," it is well to remember the context. There is a pattern here in regard to the contribution of Southerners to American success. We can see the Massachusetts agenda still working at the turn of the twentieth century when Henry Adams wrote a mean-spirited biography of Randolph of Roanoke and attempted to debunk the beautiful and true story of Captain John Smith and Pocahontas. Adams was guilty of falsehood in a deliberate, malicious effort to brand the first Southerner, Captain John Smith, as a liar.

---

[1] Manuscripts in the Simms Collection, South Caroliniana Library, University of South Carolina. Simms's quotations are from this source unless otherwise stated.

[2] *The History of South Carolina.* New and revised edition (New York: Redfield, 1860), 1-7.

[3] *Autobiography of Thomas Jefferson* (New York: Capricorn Books, 1959), 23; *Debates and Proceedings in Congress* (Washington: Gales & Seaton, 1851), 5th Congress, p. 1826 (May 26, 1798).

[4] See "The Yankee Problem in American History" and "Those People (The Yankees)" in this book. Poe lampooned New England presumptuousness brilliantly in "Boston and the Bostonians," *Broadway Journal*, November 22, 1845.

[5] Simms, "South Carolina in the Revolution" and "The Siege of Charleston" in *Southern Quarterly Review* (July and October, 1848) vol. 28:37-77. 263-327.

[6] Harlow W. Sheidley, *Sectional Nationalism: Massachusetts Conservative Leaders and the Transformation of America, 1815-1836* (Boston: Northeastern University Press, 1998).

[7] Sheidley, chapter cited.

[8] *The Papers of John C. Calhoun*, vol. 27, pp. 338-339.

# Real Causes

*An Anti-Slavery man per se cannot be elected; but a Tariff, River-and-Harbor, Pacific Railroad, Free Homestead man, may succeed although he is Anti-Slavery.*
—Horace Greeley on the 1860 Republican Convention

Review of *Clash of Extremes: The Economic Origins of the Civil War*, by Mark Egnal. New York: Hill & Wang.

---

ASK ANY TRENDY STUDENT of history today and he will tell you that without question the cause of the great American bloodletting of 1861–1865 was slavery. Slavery and nothing but slavery. The unstated and usually unconscious assumption being that only people warped by a vicious institution could possibly fight against being part of "the greatest nation on earth." This is an older corollary of the present national dictum that everybody in the world really wants to be an American if they could only be cured of delusions and bad motives — by aerial bombardment if necessary.

There is an even deeper and less conscious assumption here: malicious, unprovoked hatred of Southern people that is endemic in many American elements. Thus, according to the wisdom of current "scholars," no credit is to be given to anything that Southerners might say about their own reasons and motives. They are all merely repeating "Lost Cause myths" to cover up their evil deeds. (Of course, no one points out that "Father Abraham," the "Glorious Union," and "dying to make men free" might partake of some myth-making too.)

Set aside that the question of causation in history is a complex one, to say the least. Still it is true that historians of other generations, of vastly greater breadth of learning than most of today's, ascribed other "causes" to the most critical event in American history: clash of economic interests and cultures, blundering politicians, irresponsible agitators. There is a bit of sleight-of-hand along with today's fashionable assumptions. Even if slavery may have in some simplistic and abstract sense "caused" the *secession* of the first seven Southern States, it does not establish that it "caused" the *war*. The war was caused by the determination of Lincoln and his party to conquer the Southern states and destroy their legal governments. Caused, one might say by Northern nationalism — nationalism being a combination of romantic identification with a centralised state and interest in a unitary economic market. The *war,* after all, consisted of the invasion and conquest of the South by the U.S. government. A very simple fact that most Americans, it would seem, are unable to process, along with the plain fact that Northern soldiers did not make war for the purpose of freeing black people.

One of Lincoln's many deceptions was the claim that the Founders had intended to abolish slavery but had not quite got around to it. The Southerners of his time, thus, were rebelling against the true Founding by insisting on non-interference, while he and his party were upholding the settled understanding of the Founders. James McPherson, perhaps the "leading" historian of today in regard to the Great Unpleasantness and no Southern apologist, along with many others, points out that it was the North that had changed by 1860, while the South had remained attached to the original concept of the Union. Now one may be glad, as McPherson is, that the North changed and triumphed with a new version of America, but to deny which side was revolutionary is merely dishonest.

Historians have devoted vast attention to the South, feeling it was necessary to explain where the South went wrong, find the source of the perversion that led it to a doomed attempt to escape the greatest country on earth. For, after all, "American" is the norm of the universe and any divergence from it is a pathology. But if it was the North that changed, ought our primary focus in understanding American history to be on why and how the North changed during the pre-war period?

I pointed out twenty years ago or more that Northern history was the future cutting edge of American historical study. A large number of solid works since have proved that my prediction had some merit: Susan-Mary Grant, *North over South;* Harlow W. Sheidley, *Sectional Nationalism; Richard* F. Bensel, *Yankee Leviathan; Anne* Farrow, et al., *Complicity; Richard* H.

Abbott, *Cotton and Capital; Leonard* P. Curry, *Blueprint for Modern America;* two excellent books on Lincoln by William Marvel, and others.

*Clash of Extremes* may be counted among the works on The War that pay serious attention to the North. Writes Egnal:

> In sum, the current emphasis on slavery as the cause of the Civil War is fraught with problems. It does not clarify the sequence of events, the divisions within the sections, or the policies and actions of the Republican Party. It is these problems that a new interpretation must address.

The author does not neglect the sins of the South, real and alleged, but his most original contribution is his description of a truly critical new development of the late antebellum period, which he calls "the Lake Economy." The Midwest was first settled by Southerners farming the north side of the Ohio Valley. In the late antebellum period, the upper Midwest was settled by New Englanders and Europeans who developed a new economic regime along with a militant agenda of their own self-interest and vision of the national future. It was this culture that Lincoln and his party represented, and out of which, by military conquest, they created a new America that superseded the old Union of the Fathers and put us on the course that we follow today. It was certainly American but it was a new version that essentially repudiated the Founding.

# Those People (The Yankees)

*The North is full of tangled things...*
—G.K. Chesterton

*A meddling Yankee is God's worst creation; he cannot run his own affairs correctly, but is constantly interfering in the affairs of others, and he is always ready to repent of everyone's sins, but his own.*
—North Carolina newspaper, 1854

*The Northern onslaught upon slavery was no more than a piece of specious humbug designed to conceal its desire for economic control of the Southern States.*
—Charles Dickens, 1862

---

GENERAL LEE, with characteristic restraint, always spoke of the invaders who came to loot and destroy the South as "those people." Most Southerners then and later called them Yankees. There are several theories about the origin of the term "Yankee," but nobody knows for sure. The word has been in continual use since early colonial times, usually in an uncomplimentary way. Most likely it originated among the Dutch settlers in New Netherlands (New York) as a garbled reference to "English," designating their peculiar neighbours to the east in New England.

For a long time, right up to the War to Prevent Southern Independence,[1] "Yankee" referred specifically to New Englanders, and was used to mark them as distinct from other Americans. Not until The War, did Southerners begin to apply the term to all Northerners, who indeed had started to act like Yankees. When ambitious young "Honest Abe" Lincoln was courting popularity among his pioneer neighbours in Illinois, most of whom came from the South, he had a fund of "Yankee" stories — anecdotes and jokes about crooked peddlers and religious hypocrites from New England. When he came to town, they put the women, children, and preachers to bed, and the boys gathered around the iron stove at the local store to hear his stories.

55

The Yankee stories were popular, but not as popular as the dirty ones, for which Lincoln was regionally famous.

It is difficult to believe now, but for a long time most Americans, including most Northerners, regarded New England, not the South, as the peculiar, out-of-step section of the country. Yankees were the outsiders who thought and behaved differently from everyone else, and usually in disagreeable ways. In fact, the South, in the times of Washington, Jefferson, and Jackson, was the generally accepted model of what was "American." Remember that nine of the first twelve Presidents were Southern plantation owners.

The New York writer Washington Irving's famous 1820 story about the Headless Horseman, "The Legend of Sleepy Hollow," takes place among rural Hudson Valley people whose society could hardly be distinguished from the South. Ichabod Crane was a cowardly Yankee twit from Connecticut who presumed too far on the hospitality of the New Yorkers, so one of the young blades scared him nearly to death and sent him fleeing back to where he came from. The New York writer James Fenimore Cooper had admirable Southern characters in his novels and he despised the riffraff from New England who swarmed into the region his family had settled and developed. The New Yorker Herman Melville may well have created his fanatical Captain Ahab in *Moby Dick* as a portrait of a Yankee abolitionist. By the 1850s, however, New York (and portions of the Midwest) had been colonised by Yankees, who made up much of the state's population and were the leading newspaper editors and rich men of New York City.

Yet even as late as the eve of The War, the Democratic governor of New York, Horatio Seymour, blamed sectionalconflict on New England fanaticism, which had driven the South to secession. He declared in a public address that the attempt to stop secession by force would end in destroying the American principle of self-government. And such a war would be greatly immoral. "Upon whom are we to wage war?" Seymour asked. "Our own countrymen. . . . Their courage has never been questioned. . . .They battled by our side with equal valour in the Revolutionary struggle. . . . Virginia sent her sons, under the command of Washington, to the relief of beleaguered Boston. Alone, the South defeated the last and most desperate effort of

British power to divide our country, at the battle of New Orleans." The South had always furnished its full share of soldiers and wise and patriotic statesmen. Were Northerners to be dragooned into an ungodly war against other Americans?[2] Later, Lincoln was to find it necessary to send seasoned combat troops to New York City to control the elections and enforce the conscription of cannon fodder among the poorer classes.

At the same time and in a similar vein, a Pennsylvanian wrote: "Pennsylvania is now temporarily under the influence of Yankee politicians who have migrated thither—her leading representatives in the present Congress being adventurers from New England." Pennsylvania's misguided support for the tariff, said this commentator, "has been owing to the fact that a portion of her population were Yankee speculators in coal and iron." "In conclusion," he added, "the New England States have contributed but little to the general prosperity of the Union."[3]

George Washington had uncomplimentary things to say about New England soldiers in the War of Independence. Thomas Jefferson considered Yankees the fount of most troubles in the new Union. In 1798 Jefferson wrote "that we are completely under the saddle of Massachusetts and Connecticut, and that they ride us very hard, cruelly insulting our feelings, as well as exhausting our strength and substance." The Yankees were "marked by such a perversity of character," Jefferson added, that they were permanently divided from the rest of America.[4] Indeed, Jefferson's preference for the separation of church and state stemmed in part from his distaste for the influence exercised by the politicised Puritan preachers of New England. In numerous election sermons they portrayed Jefferson as a French Jacobin who intended to set up the guillotine and share out the women. From the beginning the Yankees were given to rhetorical extremism, something which played a large part in driving the South into secession. (For just a few out of literally thousands of examples, Waldo Emerson declaring that the inmates of the Massachusetts penitentiary were superior beings to the leaders of the South and Thoreau likening the mass murderer John Brown to Christ.)

One can understand a great deal of American history by remembering a simple fact about the founding. New England Puritans came to America to get away from a world of sinners and to construct "a shining City upon a

Hill" which would be an example for all mankind of a superior commonwealth. The Yankee elite kept all of their over-developed and self-centered righteousness after they lost their Christianity and replaced it with the imported German philosophy of Transcendentalism. By contrast, people who came to settle the South saw America as a promising garden to be cultivated, a place where land could be had and personal honour and independence be established by younger sons and common folk in ways that were no longer possible in the Mother Country.

We can see the difference starkly proved by laying side by side two diaries from the early 18th century, those of the Reverend Cotton Mather of Massachusetts and Colonel William Byrd II of Virginia. Allowing that both men were Englishmen born in the North American colonies, they could not have been more different. Mather and Byrd lived in different mental universes. While Byrd was writing in his diary about his good times (even the guilty ones), his wide reading, his socialising with cordial neighbours, his love of nature, and his adventures in the wilderness, Mather was secretly recording the evil hearts of his associates, the failure of the world to fully recognise his merit, and complaints and lectures to God about his insufficient rewards.[5]

There are "scholars" who assert that there is nothing distinctive about the South except its defense of slavery and segregation, that the South has never had any separate culture worthy of notice. Slavery existed in all the colonies and it had nothing to do with the differences in the mental worlds of Mather and Byrd, differences that obviously go back to the early days of the settlement of America. A Confederate wit captured this profound difference with the remark that The War happened because Southerners were a contented people and Yankees were not.

Another fundamental thing to understand is that the North changed radically after the founding of the United States, especially in the 1850s, while the South, though expanding over a huge territory, remained substantially the same. (What history knows as the Southern people came into being in the late 18th century with the comfortable merging of the colonial tidewater and the later settlers of the upcountry frontier.) The official view of The War tells us that Lincoln sought only to preserve the glorious old Union of the Founding Fathers, while Southerners, crazed by slavery, repudiated venerable

American principles and tried to destroy it. This is the opposite of the truth. The leaders of the South (Jefferson Davis, R.E. Lee, J.E. Johnston, and many others) were actual sons of the founding generation. They knew that their fathers had created the Union for the benefit of their own people. Southerners came to secession as they realised that being under a government controlled by people who were constantly "insulting our feelings" and "exhausting our strength and substance" defeated the purposes for which the Union had been made. Portions of the North had been waging a cold war against the South from the very beginning. As the great Southern writer William Gilmore Simms remarked, Northerners had been "fed on tiger's meat" for half a century, and it was not surprising that many were ravenous to devour the South. The North sought to convert a Union made for brotherhood and mutual benefit into a "nation" which they would dominate in their own interest.

New Englanders from the first opposed every good measure under the U.S. government and clamoured for special privileges for themselves. One of the first laws passed by the first U.S. Congress was to continue subsidising the Yankee fishing fleet as the British government had done before independence. While Virginia conquered the vast Northwest Territory and gave it to the Union for the use of all Americans, Connecticut demanded special land for itself (the Western Reserve in Ohio). New Englanders opposed the Louisiana Purchase and in general most American land acquisition and westward movement, which would mean that an ever-growing part of America would be beyond their control.

Despite all the old Western movies that portray imaginary pioneers from Boston moving west in covered wagons, New Englanders were not big hands at settling new territory until Southerners had made it safe. They decried settlers of the frontier as crude barbarians. When they moved into the Midwest they looked down on the pioneers who had preceded them there as ignorant and lazy "Hoosiers." While Southerners were exploring the Great Plains and Rocky Mountains and contending with such fierce opponents as the Mexicans and Comanche, Emerson in Massachusetts was orating about the "Self-Reliance" of the superior New England character. (Emerson got himself economically "self-reliant" for life by marrying the terminally ill daughter of a banker.) And Thoreau was celebrating bold individualism and the Great Outdoors at his little pond at Walden, in sight of the Boston smokestacks. (He did not have to work since his father was rich and Walden was close enough for home cooking and laundry as needed.) The brilliantly creative Southern writer Edgar Allan Poe referred to the self-important New England writers as "Frog-pondians," croakers who mistook their little kingdom for the world.

During the War of 1812, Yankees traded with the enemy and refused the President's constitutional call to have the militia brought into federal service. (Though for decades after the war, Massachusetts demanded that the federal government pay the expenses of the militia that had been called out but not allowed to leave the state, and demanded pensions for their "service.") During the War of 1812 Yankees talked openly of secession, something which no Southerner ever did in a time of foreign invasion. It was common knowledge that Yankees crowded the rolls of Revolutionary War pensioners by fraud or by inflating what had been 30 days peaceful militia duty into glorious war service. And then Yankee writers used their over-representation on the pension rolls to claim that the War of Independence had been fought mostly by New Englanders.[6] Southerners like Washington, John Taylor, and Nathaniel Macon refused financial rewards for their patriotic service in the war, and such heroes as Francis Marion's men and the fighters at Kings Mountain were seldom on the official rolls at all. This is not surprising since Southerners fought and sacrificed in the War of Independence for liberty and self-government while New Englanders were driven by motives of economic profit and religious bigotry.

Politically and culturally, the Yankees considered themselves to be the only true Americans. Their interests and their virtues, in their opinion, were the American standard. When young John C. Calhoun came to the House of Representatives in 1811 and made a speech about the plight of American sailors impressed by the British, a New England member scornfully called him a backwoodsman who had never seen the sea. A few years later, Yankees insisted that the government provide them with high tariffs (taxes) on imported goods so that all Americans would be forced to buy their manufactured products. This was so obviously correct (to them) that to oppose it was denounced as treason. And when Southerners pointed out the low price of cotton and the high price of goods because of the tariff, Yankees replied in Congress that all Southern economic problems were due to Southerners' well-known laziness and inferiority to New Englanders in enterprise. This arrogance is indeed a forgotten part of American history, which is usually told as if Southerners decided to secede in a fit of unprovoked hysteria over slavery. Grasping economic advantage through government is a well-known phenomenon in human affairs, but never has it been accompanied by such self-righteousness.

In the 1790s a Connecticut Puritan preacher named Jedediah Morse published the first "American" geography book. Only the title was American. Most of the book was taken up with describing the hardworking, prosperous, law-abiding, religious, and well-educated population of New England. Once you got west of the Hudson River, as Morse saw it and conveyed to the world reading public, the United States were inhabited by lazy and ignorant Germans and Scotch-Irish in the Middle States and weak and morally depraved Southerners. Pennsylvania and New Jersey fared no better than the South. New Englanders were pure Anglo-Saxons with all the exalted virtues of that race, the real Americans, the ones who counted. Curiously, Yankees take the credit for freeing the slaves, presumably because of their zeal for the equality of all mankind, but they long regarded other white Americans as people of lower or mongrel breed. That attitude has not disappeared even today. A Northeastern "intellectual" recently remarked snidely that Pennsylvania was "Philadelphia and Pittsburgh, with Mississippi in between."

It is of interest and relevance that Roman Catholics and Jews found an accepted place, sometimes a very successful place, in the South when such was unknown in the North. Today most American Catholics and Jews, who are descended from immigrants who came long after The War, join in the Yankee hue and cry against Southerners and imagine that their people have always been good Yankees (although there are notable exceptions, especially among Italian-Americans). In fact, at the time of The War, a high proportion of American Catholics and Jews were found in the South and were loyal Confederates. Nearly all the Catholics and Jews elected to public office in the U.S. were in the South (and not just Louisiana).[7] The two most famous anti-Catholic incidents in the pre-war period took place in Boston and Philadelphia, where mobs attacked and burned down convents. The local authorities connived with the mobs and few offenders were ever prosecuted.

No such incidents occurred in the South. The letters of Lincoln's supporters are full of anti-Semitic comments, and. notoriously General Grant was to banish Jews from the Union army lines.

A few years after Morse's geography was published, Noah Webster, also from Connecticut, published his "American" dictionary and spelling book. As Webster declared in a preface, his works were based upon the language of New Englanders, who spoke and spelled the purest and best English of any people in the world, including the Mother Country. Webster also introduced peculiar new spellings for a supposedly improved language — "honor" for "honour" and "exercize" for "exercise" for example. It is not widely known, but such aberrations were ignored by most Americans until The War. Some Southerners still insist on spelling real English rather than Yankee English. And Southerners naturally speak in accents close to those of Shakespeare.[8]

Noah Webster went south to sell his books. He paused in Baltimore to issue a pamphlet telling the people that they needed to be more industrious in imitation of New Englanders. Like many people at the time, he presented himself to the elder statesmen Jefferson and Madison at their plantations. This was a typical ploy of Yankee wannabe celebrities. They were received politely and thereafter promoted themselves by claiming the acquaintance and approval of the great men. What Jefferson really thought was put into a letter to James Madison in which he described Noah Webster as "a mere pedagogue of very limited understanding and very strong prejudices and party passions."

In the 1790s both Morse and Webster were critical of slavery, though their attitude contained not a trace of sympathy for black people. They thought Southern blacks did not work hard enough and were allowed to enjoy themselves too boisterously, and that they corrupted the white people by their natural immorality.

In his diary, kept on his trip to darkest Dixie, Webster wrote, "O New England! How superior are thy inhabitants in morals, literature, civility, and industry!"[9]

So far as these people were concerned "America" and New England were the same thing. They were the only Americans who counted. After their treasonous stance in the War of 1812, Yankees were in general bad favour. In response they started a deliberate and well-organised campaign for domination of the still-developing culture and identity of the United States.[10] Busy writers, journalists, schoolmarms, orators, publishers, and preachers worked to establish this domination. Among other things, they appropriated American history to themselves, even where deliberate lies were needed. Yankee historians claimed that the South had not contributed to the Revolutionary War but had only been saved by New England soldiers. Daniel Webster, the great defender of "the Union," while a guest in Charleston, orated about the many graves of New England soldiers who had died fighting in the South. The trouble was, those graves did not exist. While many Southern volunteers had served in the North, no New England unit had ever served in the South, where all the important fighting took place after the first few years. (Tory regiments from Connecticut and New York did serve in the Southern campaigns.) Thus the Yankees tried to convert the successful War of Independence, which should have been a source of mutual celebration and unity for all Americans, into their exclusive property. Yet American history is told as the story of patriotic New England defenders of "the nation" versus wicked Southern sectionalists.

To a great extent the Yankee program of dominance succeeded in ways that last into the 21st century. Even today most Americans know all about how the country began with the "Pilgrim Fathers" at Plymouth and little about Jamestown (the site of the first lasting settlement and the real First Thanksgiving). They know all about Paul Revere and next to nothing of the vital history of the War of Independence in the South. Likewise, the Yankees made a claim on the "West." *The Oregon Trail* is still cited as a classic of the American frontier. It was by a wealthy tourist from Boston and is entirely about Yankee settlers in the Pacific Northwest, ignoring 95 per cent of the exciting story of the frontier, which was a predominantly Southern enterprise. By the 1850s, the migration of Yankees into New York and the upper Midwest had spread the campaign for cultural domination over much of the North. Only the hated South consistently ignored or openly disdained Yankee claims of superiority.

What aroused the Yankee's antipathy to Southern society was its opposition to his pride and his profits, which in his mind were no more than his due as the only true American. The hostile critique of the South was a product of a self-absorbed New England culture that felt itself to be vastly superior to the rest of the United States but at the same time believed itself to be deprived of its rightful mastership of American destiny. It was in considerable measure a response by New England leadership to having been challenged and defeated by Jeffersonian and Jacksonian republicanism led by Southerners. The rise of the Republican Party in the 1850s and its war of conquest against the South in the 1860s and 1870s were in a sense the belated assertion of Yankee supremacy, as many Northerners recognised at the time, with approval or disapproval. Resistance to New England dominion was explained, in true Puritan fashion, by the Southerner's evil nature — his lack of the Yankee virtues of self-discipline, order, morality, schooling, and industry. Association with Southerners, white and black, at times seemed almost to put the Yankee in danger of personal contamination. One cannot help but detect in these people some intimations of envy and an attempt to cover up a feeling of inferiority.

This New England hatred of the South was fully developed before slavery became an issue and only marginally if at all reflected antislavery sentiment. At the time of the Revolutionary War, slaves were found in all 13 colonies and their numbers had actually been increasing in the North. The North did not have tobacco, sugar, and cotton plantations, but slaves were to be found on the larger farms and as domestic servants in affluent families. Ten per cent of the population of New York City were slaves. The great Massachusetts heroes John Hancock and Sam Adams brought some of their black bondsmen with them when they came to Philadelphia to sign the Declaration of Independence. Such Northern heroes of the Revolution as General Jacob Herkimer of New York and Frederick and Peter Muhlenberg of Pennsylvania, among many others, were slave-owners, as were a majority of the Northern delegates to the Philadelphia convention that drew up the Constitution of the United States. Into the early 1800s slavery was not only found in the Northern states, it was commonplace and unremarked.

The facts about slavery in the North have always been well-established. When Northerners suffer from shock at learning some of the facts, they only prove how self-deceptive they have been about their own history.

# The Yankee Problem

Timothy Dwight was the President of Yale University, a hater of Jefferson, and one of the "Connecticut Wits," a group of writers who flourished in the 1790s and considered themselves (with presumptuous inaccuracy) to be the founders of American literature. In a long poem celebrating the new America, he included a passage about the slaves in Connecticut (where at the time the percentage of slaveholding families in the population was equal to that of the South in 1860):

*But kindly fed, and clad, and treated he*
*Slides on thro' life, with more than common glee.*
*For here mild manners good to all impart,*
*And stamp with infamy the unfeeling heart;*
*Here law, from vengeful rage, the slave defends;*
*And here the gospel peace on earth extends.*

Oh, how happy to be a slave in Connecticut!

When John C. Calhoun and other Southerners went to Yale to study in the early 19th century they did not move from a land of slavery to a land of freedom, as was later claimed. Dwight continued on in his lame verse to describe by contrast the horrors that were the lot of slaves elsewhere, with absurdly exaggerated descriptions of "cracking whips and dying groans," torture, cannibalism, and bashing out babies' brains before their grieving parents. (Though he seems to refer to the West Indies rather than the Southern States.) In the same poem Dwight manages to paint a pretty picture of slavery among his own and anticipates by several decades the lurid abolitionist shock descriptions of the South that began to be broadcast in the 1830s.

The typical New England attitude toward slavery before the rise of abolitionism in the 1830s was expressed by the elder statesman John Adams. In the early period of the Union he wrote that argument about slavery was a dispute about words, not substance. Adams said "that in some countries the labouring poor were called freemen, in others they were called slaves, but that the difference as to the state was imaginary only.... That the condition of the labouring poor in most countries, that of the fishermen particularly in the Northern States, is as abject as that of the slaves." Many years later Adams had not changed his opinion. In one of his last letters to Jefferson, during the Missouri controversy, which alarmed both of the elder statesmen, he wrote: "I have been so terrified with this phenomenon that I constantly said in former times to the Southern gentlemen, I must leave it to you. I will vote for no measure against your judgments."[11] Despite this, the recent television docudrama about John Adams portrays the plain, manly patriot John Adams contending about slavery with a mincing fop from South Carolina. The Yankee moral self-congratulation at the expense of Southerners never ends.

John Quincy Adams spent his last years doing exactly what his father had warned against—agitating relentlessly about slavery in the South and declaiming that an evil Southern "slave power" dominated the Union and threatened the values and interests of the decent people of the North. However, he did so only AFTER Southern opposition had made him into a bitter, beleaguered one-term President and he no longer had any hope of national preferment. (John Quincy Adams, by the way, was not in real life the cuddly teddy bear played by Anthony Hopkins in the movie "Amistad." He was hateful and vindictive, as any glance at his portraits or his diary will show.)

The gradual disappearance of slavery (and black people) during the early 19th century by no means ended the Northern involvement with slavery. Northern investors were prominent among the owners of the very lucrative sugar plantations in Louisiana before The War, and others acquired the plantations of absent Confederates after the war began (one of the reasons that Lincoln exempted southern Louisiana from the Emancipation Proclamation).

More importantly, New England shippers, right up to The War, were major players in the international slave trade, along with the Spanish and Portuguese. Bringing people from Africa for sale in the insatiable slave markets of Cuba and Brazil was illegal for American citizens but too profitable to resist — one voyage could make a shipper's fortune. Numerous wealthy New Englanders were invested in this business, including a close friend and political bankroller of that great defender of the North, Daniel Webster of Massachusetts and the founder of Rhode Island's Brown University. After 1808, no slaves could be legally imported into the United States. Southerners mostly were in favour of this. The black population was proliferating mightily by natural increase (a sign of good treatment) and there was no demand for importation despite the bringing of vast new lands into cultivation. Diverted from their American market, the Yankees continued the slave trade where there were still buyers. (Some of them also were able to cut into the British monopoly of the opium trade to China.)

The future Confederate General Henry A. Wise, while he was U.S. Minister to Brazil, the future Confederate General James Conner, while he was U.S. District Attorney in Charleston, and the future Confederate Navy hero John N. Maffitt, while he commanded a U.S. vessel in the Caribbean, were zealous in interdicting and prosecuting Americans illegally engaged in the international slave trade, but found that cases were usually transferred to the Northern point of origin of the voyage, where Northern juries refused to convict. And to pour yet more into the overflowing cup of Yankee hypocrisy, some New Englanders continued to own slave sugar plantations in Cuba even after emancipation in the United States. [12]

Black people were not encouraged, before or after The War, to settle in the North or West. It has been shown that the fabled Underground Railroad was mostly just that, a fable made up after the fact when it was safe to *have been* a brave antislavery worker. Sometimes the Underground Railroad involved slave stealing for resale rather than slave freeing. [13] On the other hand, right up to the war, Southern family slaves accompanied masters to such Northern resorts as Saratoga Springs, to Montreal, and to the Western gold and silver mines, and returned home again. Though the number of black people in the "free States" was negligible, their segregated, impoverished, illiterate, disease- and crime-ridden communities (as shown plainly by the Census) offered little attraction. In 1860 there more free black people living in the South than in the North. Many in the South were comfortably off and some were rich and plantation owners themselves. [14]

Historians and commentators have created a vast literature and many theories about why the South has been so peculiar, so out-of-step and contrary in the history of the United States. Their unexamined assumption is that the North is and always has been the standard for "America" and normality. Southerners, who fought to separate from "the greatest nation on earth" must surely be psychologically warped (the pseudo-scientific version) if not irredeemably evil (the righteous version). But as we noted earlier, Governor Seymour (and he was far from alone among thoughtful people in the North) considered the strange and evil thing to be that so many Northerners had come to support a government that would invade, loot, burn-out, and kill their Southern fellow citizens, destroy legitimate state governments, and rule a large part of the population by force, contrary to all previous American understanding and in violation of the most fundamental American principle — consent of the governed

Indeed, the great untold story of American history is Yankee history. It is Yankee, not Southern, history that needs to be put under the microscope for further analysis. How did the post-Puritan North move from John Adams to John Brown and Abraham Lincoln? How to describe and explain of the vast changes that took place in Northern society between the Revolution and Lincoln's election? For Lincoln and his party to take power and inaugurate a war of conquest against the South was a new and revolutionary development even in terms of Northern history.

Most of the founders and prominent leaders of the Republican party in all the Northern States, other than Lincoln himself, were natives of New England; Horace Greeley and William Cullen Bryant, the leading Republican editors in New York City, Thaddeus Stevens, the leading Radical Republican of Pennsylvania (who, thanks to the tariff, made $6,000 profit on every mile of railroad iron sold by his foundry); Senators Salmon P. Chase and Benjamin F. Wade in Ohio, Zachariah Chandler in Michigan, Lyman Trumbull in Illinois (along with Stephen A. Douglas, a Democrat who betrayed his many Southern supporters by urging Northern Democrats to back Lincoln's war). Many other Republican stalwarts were born in the Yankee-dominated region of upstate New York, known throughout the United States as "the Burnt-Over District" because it had been swept by so many waves of fanaticism.

An important ingredient in the formation of a new militant North was the decline of orthodox Christianity. The strict Calvinism under which New England had been founded had deteriorated constantly almost from the beginning. The Adamses were already Unitarians by the 1820s. In the 1830s orthodoxy was further shattered by new intellectual currents released by the French Revolution in Europe — especially newly-influential German philosophy and Biblical criticism. Emerson went from Massachusetts to Germany to study. There he learned that mankind was engaged in a dialectical process of progress that would lead eventually to the removal of all evils and contradictions from history — to the perfection of society. He returned home, resigned from the Congregational clergy, and announced that "whatever is old corrupts." This included the Christian sacraments, which were to be discarded as relics of barbarism. Yankees have always prided themselves on being trendy thinkers.

Soon he was declaring that "the American" (by which, of course, he meant the New Englander) was "a New Man," one destined to be the cutting edge of humanity's progress. The new doctrine made large inroads into the New England intelligentsia. When the breakdown of orthodox Christianity reached the less educated masses of Yankees, it took a different but parallel direction. "The Burnt-Over District," the upstate New York region settled by the overflow of the poorer population from the Yankee States, was struck by wave after wave of hysterical revivalism, as were similar areas of the Midwest. From this social turmoil, reminiscent in its effects of that which struck the United States in the 1960s, emerged a new post-millennial religion: America was a uniquely virtuous land with a uniquely special relationship with God. Indeed, America + Democracy = God. Such was the underlying assumption and often the declared doctrine of sermons and political speeches from that day to this.[15]

Emerson's future state of perfection and God's plan for humanity had been conflated with America's chosenness. From the point of view of Christianity, the "American" belief is heresy. From the point of view of history, it is nonsense. But it is powerful enough that it can make any politician quickly into a crowd-pleaser. A receptive public to this day applauds presidential declarations that America is the model of perfection to which all the world wishes, or should wish, to conform. That there is an American mission to spread the perfection of "democratic capitalism" to all humanity. The South was the first victim of such distorted Christian faith, but it has even made headway among Southerners during the 20th century of world wars.

The intensity of emotional and religious upheaval in the Burnt-Over District was high. That small area of New York State, within the space of twenty years or so, saw: Joseph Smith receive a new book of scripture from the angel Moroni and found the polygamous Mormon church; William Miller begin the Seventh Day Adventists by predicting (inaccurately) the end of the world; the flourishing of spiritualism ("spirit rapping"); the free love colony of John Humphrey Noyes at Oneida; the first feminist convention held at Seneca Falls; and John Brown, who was born in Connecticut, collecting accomplices and financial backers for his terrorist expeditions. (One of the financial backers in the Burnt-Over District was Gerritt Smith, one of the richest men in the country, who checked himself into a lunatic asylum when his connection with Brown was exposed. Other prominent Brown bankrollers took vacations in Canada.)

For those inspired by the new faith, anything that stood in the way of American perfection must be stamped out. The problem to be attacked and eradicated was at various times identified as the Catholic church, the Masons, meat-eating, liquor, and marriage, all of which engendered earnest campaigns for their elimination from American life. Clearly many Yankees were discontented people looking for something or someone to blame for the uneasiness they felt as their society suffered through religious breakdown, industrialisation with its accompanying dislocation and periodic unemployment, and a flood of non-Anglo-Saxon, non-Protestant immigrants. By the later 1830s the reformist frenzy had fixed upon slavery, by now limited to the Southern states and territories. It was already well-established that Southerners were an alien, lazy, violent people, lacking the sober virtues of Northerners.

Most Americans, including many Southerners, had long thought slavery not an altogether good thing and wished that it had never come to America. Nevertheless, most understood that, as Jefferson put it, "we have the wolf by the ears," and no quick solution was to be had. (Lincoln himself said that he would not know what to do about slavery even if he had the power, which he at first denied having.) The abolitionism flooding forth from parts of the North in sermons, orations, newspapers, schoolbooks, broadsides, slanderous petitions, and pamphlets in the 1830s was something new and different. It had little interest in the welfare of black people, nor even the in bad effects of slavery on the American economy that had been argued (erroneously) by earlier critics. Slave-holding was a SIN, a blot on the perfection of what was now regarded not as the Union but as a "nation" with a divine mission. Abolitionists preached vividly that every evil they could imagine as a potential abuse by a slave-owner was a fact of everyday life in the South, of which they were completely ignorant.[16]

Abolitionist propaganda served the purpose of emotional identity for many Yankees and of pornography for others. Yankee imaginings of sexual misbehaviour in the South were of the same source as similar imaginings that had led to the burning of convents. The great abolitionist preacher Henry Ward Beecher (brother of Mrs. Stowe of *Uncle Tom's Cabin),* got rich and famous from staging mock slave auctions where young, nearly-white women were put on the block. He was later exposed for seducing young married women of his congregation, and was so involved in smuggling arms to abolitionists in Kansas that rifles were known there as "Beecher's Bibles."

Southerners found themselves regularly and publically denounced in the harshest and vilest terms, as barbarians, pirates, kidnappers, evil, tyrannical men lacking every American and Christian virtue. It is significant that the orthodox clergy of the North looked unfavourably on the new currents. Northern Catholic and Episcopal bishops and Presbyterian theologians plainly denounced and warned against the hysterical propaganda of the abolitionists. Episcopal Bishop John Henry Hopkins of Vermont said in 1863, even as The War had raged on: "The South has done more than any people on earth for the African race." One could make several large books just discussing the Northern condemnation of what was deemed the fanatical and meddling spirit of New Englanders. A prominent New York Democratic writer hit the nail on the head: "The Abolitionists have throughout committed the fatal mistake of urging a purely moral cause by means, not only foreign to that character, but hostile to it, incompatible with it. Where they had to persuade, they have undertaken to force. Where love was the spirit in which they should have approached the task, they have done it in that of hate."[17]

Abolitionism, looked at as it actually was, had more to do with hatred of the slave-holder and then of the whole Southern white population than it did with black welfare. It was an inappropriate and destructive response to the problem of slavery in the United States, as the more conservative elements of the North understood. Daniel Webster, the greatest man of the North, said, during the debates leading to the Compromise of 1850, that Southerners would have gradually eliminated slavery if it had not been for the abolitionist frenzy. But the relentless propaganda grew steadily. By 1860 there was a Northern generation that had grown up knowing nothing about their Southern fellow countrymen except abolitionist propaganda. And vast numbers of recent immigrants, ignorant of American history and the Constitution, were highly susceptible. By that time, the most thoughtful and perceptive Southern clergy of all denominations were convinced that the North was given over to heresy and atheism and that secession was a religious as well as a political necessity.

In New York City in 1860 there were women and children working 16 hour days for starvation wages, 150,000 unemployed, 40,000 homeless, 600 brothels (some with girls as young as 10), and 9,000 grog shops where the poor could temporarily drown their sorrows. Half of the children of the city did not live past the age of five. And at the same time there were ostentatiously rich men who kept race horses and mistresses, dined every day at Delmonicos, and lit their cigars with fifty dollar banknotes. Many Southerners had been to New York. Some had seen the slums of London. When a Southern plantation owner looked over the land, the living, and the people he had inherited, and his and their daily life, and examined his conscience, he was not inclined to accept the malicious charges of people who wanted to destroy his way of life at no cost to themselves. Southern opinion of "those people" did not improve when the invading armies showed little regard for the lives and property of civilians, black or white, and for the then well-recognised rules of warfare between civilised nations.

Yankees did not like for their superiority to be called into question, then or later. But Southerners were a proud people who thought for themselves. John Tyler, father of the future President, remarked in the 1790s that "the Northern cattle" seemed bent on besmirching the honourable reputation of Virginia. In the 1850s, George Washington Harris, a Tennessee River steamboat captain and one of the many excellent, under-rated writers of the Old South, had his rambunctious character "SutLovingood," give a disquisition on "The Puritan Yankee." Sut summed Yankees up as "powerfullornary stock." Knowledgeable Europeans, then and later, shared a similar view. They provide a useful objective perspective on the two sides in the War to Prevent Southern Independence because they do not automatically take at face value the Yankees' assumption that they are invariably nobly motivated in everything they do.[18]

In a Union as vast, constantly expanding, and diverse as the United States in the mid-19th century, there was bound to be conflict among different regions with different interests and ways of life. But such conflicts need not lead automatically to the bloodiest and most destructive war of that century. What made war nearly inevitable was the rise in the North of an aggressive party that regarded the Southern states with animosity and was determined to rule ruthlessly in the interests of the North. Many Republican politicians, editors, and eggheads expressed this intention publicly and boastfully and with malice aforethought. Everyone understood this to be the case in 1860, even though Lincoln occasionally made conciliatory noises about his inoffensive intentions, which later historians have taken at face value. Lincoln won the Presidency with the support of only two-fifths of the people, but his party had a majority in the North and was about to assume power to carry out its agenda by control over all the force and patronage of the federal government.[19]

In 1860 antislavery sentiment in itself was not sufficient to win an election, much less to inaugurate a war of conquest. There had to be other developments to bring Lincoln and his party to power. Described briefly, these included an impulse toward "national greatness" (a product of both economic interests and emotions), with the "nation," of course, understood as the North; the rise of an aggressive class of industrial and banking moguls in New York and in the Great Lakes corridor of Buffalo, Pittsburgh, Cleveland, Detroit, and Chicago; the arrival in the Midwest of radical, power-worshiping Germans fleeing the failed revolutions of 1848, to provide a militant nucleus of ideologues, activists, and soldiers for the Republicans; and Lincoln's clever manipulation of a phony but powerful issue: the "extension of slavery."

Let us give the last word to a Confederate soldier who was an unwilling guest of "those people" as a prisoner of war. When he got back home he wrote up his impressions for his hometown Georgia newspaper:

> They believed their manners and customs more enlightened, their intelligence and culture immeasurably superior. Brimful of hypocritical cant and puritan ideas, they preach, pray and whine. The most parsimonious of wretches, they extoll charity...the worst of dastards, they are the most selfish of men, they are the most blatant philanthropists. The blackest-hearted hypocrites, they are religious fanatics.
>
> They are agitators and schemers, braggarts and deceivers, swindlers and extortions, and yet pretend to Godliness, truth, purity and humanity. The shibboleth of their faith is, "The Union must and shall be preserved," and they hold on to this with all the peculiar obstinacy of their nature.
>
> They say we are all benighted people, and are trying to pull down that which God himself built up. Many of these bigots express astonishment at finding the majority of our men could read and write, they have actually been educated to regard the Southern people as grossly illiterate, and little better than savages. The whole nation lives, breathes and prospers in delusions; and their chiefs control the spring of the social and political machine with masterly hands.
>
> They are so entirely incongruous to our people that they and their descendants will ever be our natural enemies.[20]

This Confederate soldier's sentiments are the same as Jefferson's 60 years before, except that now they cover the entire North and not just Massachusetts and Connecticut.

---

[1] The proper name for the American war of 1861–1865 has always been a subject of argument. Dr. Charles T. Pace of Greenville, North Carolina, in

his study of the war (*The War for Southern Independence" Why War?* Shotwell Publishing, 2015) has put forward the term "War to Prevent Southern Independence." This is the most precisely accurate term that has ever been used. I have adopted it and other writers have followed suit.

[2] *Public Record: Including Speeches, Messages. . . . of Horatio Seymour* (New York: 1868). A rich collection of commentary on the era of The War by an antiwar Democrat. Seymour was actually a relative moderate in the ranks of Lincoln's Northern critics.

[3] *The African Race in the North and the South, Being a Correspondence between Two Pennsylvanians* (London: Bradbury & Evans, 1861).

[4] Thomas Jefferson to John Taylor, June 1, 1798.

[5] Richard M. Weaver, "Two Diarists," in *In Defense of Tradition: Collected Shorter Writings of Richard M. Weaver,* ed. Ted J. Smith III (Indianapolis: 2000), pp. 720-748.

[6] Clyde Wilson, "'Tiger's Meat': William Gilmore Simms and the History of the Revolution," *Simms Review,* vol. 8 (2000), pp. 22-31.

[7] Robert N. Rosen, *The Jewish Confederates* (Columbia, S.C.: 2000); Kelly J. O'Grady, *Clear the Confederate Way! . . .* (Mason City, Iowa: 1999).

[8] Dr. James E. Kibler, emeritus professor of English at the University of Georgia, is the leader of this movement. See also Clyde Wilson, "Shakespeare Spoke Southern," www.abbevilleinstitute.org.

[9] Noah Webster's adventures in the South are fully recounted in Harry R. Warfel, ed., *Letters of Noah Webster* (New York: 1953), and in Warfel, *Noah Webster: Schoolmaster to America* (New York: 1936).

[10] See Harlow W. Sheidley, *Sectional Nationalism: Massachusetts Conservative Leaders and the Transformation of America. . . .* (Boston: 1998).

[11] Jefferson in his autobiography summarized Adams's comments about the 3/5ths compromise in the Constitution. The later remarks in John Adams to Thomas Jefferson, February 3, 1821.

[12] Clyde Wilson, "Spielberg's *Amistad,*" in Wilson, *Defending Dixie. . . .* (Columbia, SC: 2006), pp. 179-183.

[13] Larry Gara, *The Liberty Line: The Legend of the Underground Railroad* (Lexington, KY: 1996). The "Underground Railroad" has spawned enough recent literature to fill a small library, much of it directed at children and produced by the U.S. government, although it is an insignificant and dubious portion of the "history" of slavery in the U.S. The ultimate absurdity is the placing of the likeness of Harriet Tubman on U.S. currency.

[14] Ervin L. Jordan, Jr., *Black Confederates and Afro-Yankees in Civil War Virginia* (Charlottesville: 1995); Larry Koger, *Black Slaveowners: Free Black Slavemasters in South Carolina* (Columbia, SC: 1994); Gary B. Mills, *The Forgotten People: Cane River's Creoles of Color* (Baton Rouge: 1977).

[15] Ernest Lee Tuveson, *Redeemer Nation: The Idea of America's Millennial Role* (Chicago: 1968).

[16] Avery O. Craven, *The Coming of the Civil War* (Chicago: 1966), chapters 1-7.

[17] This statement was made by John O'Sullivan of New York, editor of *The Democratic Review* and one of the most prominent Northern spokesmen of the Democratic Party during the 1840s and 1850s. He could not stomach Lincoln's war against the South and was about to leave for Europe, where he defended the Confederacy. A number of Northerners went to Europe for the same reason. The painter James McNeill Whistler was one.

[18] Charles Adams, *Slavery, Secession, and Civil War: Views from the United Kingdom and Europe, 1856—1865* (Lanham, MD: 2007), an invaluable collection.

[19] See Marc Egnal, *Clash of Extremes: The Economic Origins of the Civil War* (New York: 2009); William Marvel, *Mr. Lincoln Goes to War* (Boston: 2006).

[20] Published in the Smyrna, Georgia, *Bugle Call* in 1864 and widely reprinted in Southern papers.

# The Yankee Victorious: Why and How

*The flag which he [my grandfather, Francis Scott Key] had then so proudly hailed, I saw waving at the same place over the victims of as vulgar and brutal despotism as modern times have witnessed.*
—Francis Key Howard, a prisoner of Lincoln at Fort McHenry, 1861

*Slavery is no more the cause of this war than gold is the cause of robbery.*
—Governor Joel Parker of New Jersey, 1863

*It always makes me proud of my country to see all those fine young men in the U.S. Army.*
—Crooked Yankee banker in the classic film "Stagecoach"

---

AMONG "THOSE PEOPLE," as General Lee called the invading Yankees, the antislavery sentiment of some Northerners was never in itself sufficient to support the election of a Republican president, much less a war of invasion and conquest of the Southern people by the federal government. Other and more powerful interests lay behind the rise of the Republican Party. The most important of these interests were capitalists who wished to use the federal government in numerous ways to enhance their wealth (which they presented as necessary to the prosperity and progress of the whole country). Their schemes had long been hamstrung by the Constitutional scruples and small government principles of the majority of Southern congressmen who held to the Jeffersonian preference for a small, inexpensive, and unobtrusive government

The most fundamental American political division had been revealed in the conflict of Jefferson and Hamilton in the first days of the U.S. government. Jeffersonians, largely though not entirely Southern, believed that the "consent of the governed" found its bottom-line in the will of the people of each State, that the federal government was one of specific and limited authority explicit in the Constitution, and in general that government governed best when it governed least and, unlike the monarchies of the Old World, left the people to peacefully enjoy the fruits of their labour.

From the beginning Hamiltonians, largely affluent Northerners, had seen the federal government as a tool, the powers and activities of which were to be stretched and expanded at every opportunity, and the Constitution as a spring-board of power that was to be reinterpreted at will. The government should be used to develop the American Union into a great and rich "nation" by encouragement of profitable business enterprise in the manner of the British Empire. Such a government would in their view strengthen the country and increase general prosperity through policies that would, not incidentally, further empower and enrich influential Northern-centered interests. [1]

Fundamental to these conflicts was a basic regional division in the American economy. The South produced the immense majority of foreign exports — tobacco, cotton, rice, sugar — without which there could have been no foreign trade. Part of the Northern economy was mercantile—involved with the carrying trade in Southern products. But after the War of 1812 the Northern economy was increasingly industrialised as an outlet for surplus capital and population. That economy could produce nothing that was not produced by the more advanced British industry.

Northern industrialists thought they needed tariffs (taxes) on imports so that the price of British goods would be raised and Northern goods could be sold at great profit for just a little less than the taxed imports. This was presented as the "American System," a boon to the whole country, purportedly increasing the wealth and strength of the "nation."

Thoughtful Southerners quickly perceived that the tariff forced them to pay higher than market prices for manufactured goods and, by discouraging reciprocal trade, depressed the European market for Southern produce. Why should Northerners sell their products in a home market artificially protected by the government, while the price of cotton, on which so much of the national economy depended, was decided in an open world market over which the producers had no control? "Why should the government pay the expenses of one set of men and not of another?" asked John C. Calhoun. He further pointed out that the benefits of the "American System" went entirely to the wealthy class of the North and not to Americans in general. Besides, the Constitution allowed the federal government to levy tariffs in order to support itself, not to provide unconstitutional favours to some people at the expense of others.[2]

New Englanders, with their customary arrogance, attempted to disguise their greed by claiming that the South was poor and backward, low prices for its products being due entirely to its own laziness and ignorance. This absurdity has been repeated endlessly by historians. In fact, the South was prosperous and produced the greater part of the wealth of the country. Southerners did not go in for industry in a big way because their agricultural life was more profitable and congenial. The most important innovation of the pre-war period, the McCormick reaper, though manufactured in the Midwest where it was needed, was invented by a Southerner, as were other important items. Through the leadership of scientific farmers like Edmund Ruffin, the worn-out lands of the older Southern States had been restored to productivity before The War. When it became necessary to repel invasion, Confederate scientists and engineers, professional and amateur, performed miracles of industrial production and technological innovation. The "backwardness" of the South was entirely in the eye of the hostile beholder.[3]

From the War of 1812 up to the Polk administration of 1844-1849, U.S. politics had consisted largely of conflict between Jeffersonian and Hamiltonian policies, as indicated by continuing inconclusive struggles over the national bank, national debt, federal expenditures, the tariff, subsidised "internal improvements," and the disposition of the vast public domain of western lands. By the later 1840s Polk and the Democratic Party had seemingly settled many of these questions. In the Walker Tariff of 1846 taxes on imports had been brought down to a level that did not force Americans to pay higher prices to politically-favoured Northeastern manufacturers. Polk's Independent Treasury had seemed to kill off the "national bank" project for good, establishing the long-desired Jeffersonian goal of separating the control of the currency from the power and profit of private banking interests. And the President had vetoed as unconstitutional a multi-million dollar "Rivers and Harbours" bill which had contemplated federal subsidy of hundreds of local "improvement" boondoggles, largely for the Great Lakes States.

Polk's Democrats were a little more prone to rely on the manipulation of political machinery and more ready to go to war than Jefferson had been; but, as in the Louisiana Purchase and Florida acquisition, Jeffersonians had always been alert to expanding American borders where there were potential foreign threats. The successful Mexican War was acquiring vast new undeveloped and sparsely settled territory for homes for future generations of Americans, and had canceled the threat that any European imperial power could occupy the Pacific coast. Calhoun, the most far-seeing and fair-minded leader of the time, warned Americans to settle for these gains and not take the road to further conquest and imperialism, to the "Manifest Destiny" that many were touting. More territory was forbidden fruit that would poison American republicanism.

Alas, the Democratic Party triumph over Hamiltonianism in the 1840s was to be short-lived. Towards the end of the war, David Wilmot of Pennsylvania introduced into the House of Representatives what was to become known as "the Wilmot Proviso." Wilmot had supported the administration's tariff reductions, to the disfavour of his iron-industry State, and was anxious to regain some favour at home. The Wilmot Proviso said that slavery would not be legal in any of the huge territory to be acquired by the ongoing war with the Mexican dictator Santa Anna. The ground had been prepared by Northern anger over the blocked rent-seeking agenda and by a furor a few years earlier against the admission of the independent Republic of Texas to the Union. This furor had persuaded much of the Northern public, especially the fourth made up of the foreign-born, that when Northerners moved west it was a mission to settle a continent and when Southerners moved west it was a diabolical conspiracy to spread slavery.

The measure, which President Polk decried as politically motivated, unnecessary, and dangerous,[4] was quickly passed in the House by a resentful Northern majority, failed in the Senate, and was passed again by the House the next year. The measure clearly violated the Missouri Compromise line, widely regarded as sacred, which had heretofore been applied to all new territory. A few years later, the proponents of the Proviso policy would dishonestly erupt in hysteria claiming that Southerners had overthrown the sacred Missouri Compromise by the Kansas-Nebraska acts which allowed the people of any territory to vote to legalise slavery if they chose. (Even though

81

the Kansas-Nebraska acts resulted not from Southern demands but from the machinations of Northern politicians.)

For Southerners, the passage of the Proviso by a Northern majority meant that the long tacit agreement to share new territory between the North and South would soon be abrogated. There would be no more Southern States and the South would become a permanent minority to be governed by hostile interests — in the Union that had been founded by their fathers and grandfathers for their protection and well-being. This in fact was exactly what the predominant interests of the North wanted. It was particularly galling to the South since everyone was well aware that it was Southern statesmanship and Southern military courage that had been responsible for almost all the expansion of American territory.

When the Wilmot Proviso broke upon the country, Southerners had been going about their daily lives, those who were not in Mexico exhibiting their American patriotism in arms. Southerners had no agenda for "spreading slavery." But they deeply resented the implied offense to their honour and apprehended the effects of an obviously hostile Northern majority. And in their view of the Constitution, the legality or prohibition of slavery was to be decided by the American peoples who would create new sovereign States in the acquired region, when (or after) those sovereign States came into being.

The crisis created by the Wilmot Proviso was supposedly settled by a cobbled together politicians' creation known as "the Compromise of 1850," which most Southerners accepted hopefully in the interest of peace. The two great national leaders Henry Clay and Daniel Webster denounced abolitionists and urged Northerners to settle on a compromise and save the Union, the latter sacrificing his Northern popularity by his plea for moderation. In a last great speech, a few weeks before his death, the other great national elder statesman, Calhoun, told the Senate and the country that this compromise was useless because it did not touch the basic issue. While the South considered it a settlement in good faith, he said, for the now dominant forces in the North it was only as a stepping stone to further demands and concessions. The Union to which he had devoted his life would frightfully dissolve in the near future, probably in the wake of a presidential election.

A furor over "the extension of slavery" had arisen which, coupled with strengthening Northern resentment at the Southern obstruction of capitalist-favoured legislation, would end a little over a decade later in the seizure of the White House by a new party, the Republicans, elected entirely by Northern votes and boastfully and forthrightly dedicated to Northern economic interests and to making sure that all new territory would be "Free Soil," the exclusive domain of white men — black people, slave or free, forever excluded.   Thus the years before Lincoln's election were embroiled in controversy over the question of the status of future States.   The hysterical political style of the North (as described in my previous article), encouraged by the cynical propaganda of ambitious politicians, converted Southern insistence on equality in the territories into a diabolical campaign by a ruthless "Slave Power" or "Slavocracy" to dominate the country and even to enslave Northern whites.

While The War was not "about" slavery, it is true that heated conflict over the "extension" or "expansion" of slavery marked American politics in the years leading up to secession.   This issue, and the relative behaviour of North and South in regard to it, is complicated and has more often than not been misrepresented by historians.   Let us try to make sense of what led up to the Wilmot Proviso and then, without too much complicated legislative detail, what happened after.

In 1785 the Continental Congress adopted a measure preventing slavery in the huge Northwest Territory that had been conquered by Virginia and given for the use of the citizens of all the States.   The measure was drafted by Jefferson and had the support of most of the South.   This was before the Constitution was ratified and at a time when the possibility of bringing in many thousands more African slaves to work new lands was wide open.   For many reasons, almost nobody wanted that.

The further importation of slaves into the United States was forbidden in 1808, with Southern approval.   The issues and conditions had changed in 1819 when Missouri, settled largely by people from Virginia, North Carolina, and Kentucky, wrote its constitution and applied for admission to the Union. A Northern majority in the House of Representatives attempted to bar the admission of Missouri on the grounds that its constitution allowed slavery.

(Kentucky, Tennessee, Alabama, and Mississippi, along with Louisiana from the Louisiana Purchase, had already been admitted with slavery. The treaty with France had required that private property of the French inhabitants in the Purchase be respected.)

President Monroe and his cabinet and the elder statesmen Jefferson and Madison immediately recognised for what it was this attempt to bar the sovereign people of Missouri from the Union under the constitution they had written. It was a cynical play for power, to rally elements of the North against the Southern Jeffersonians who had ruled for two decades and to dilute future Southern influence.[5]

Eventually there was a compromise, carried by the South and a few friendly Northerners, that admitted Missouri with a constitution drawn up by its citizens, but stipulated that a line would be drawn through the remainder of the Louisiana Purchase above which slavery would not be legal during territorial status. There was no active emancipation involved in either the Northwest Ordinance or the Missouri Compromise, and many people visited and even remained considerable periods in the upper region with their slaves. In the 1820s Illinois seriously considered the legalisation of slave-holding.

The Missouri controversy darkened Jefferson's last years. Jefferson had always thought slavery a bad thing and wished something could be done about it. But the sovereignty of the people of the States was more vital than the intractable matter of the black slaves. Jefferson said the conflict was "a fire-bell in the night" that was "the death-knell" of the American Union. He was not referring to slavery as the danger that would destroy the Union, contrary to what has often been asserted. The danger to the Union was not slavery, which had long existed, but the attempt of the North to dictate to the people of a sovereign State the nature of its society. A few years later, in the last months of his life, Jefferson recommended that Virginia once more assert sovereignty and nullify unconstitutional federal "internal improvements" legislation.[6]

And Jefferson pointed out an important consideration that was conveniently forgotten in later controversies and overlooked by historians. The Northern attempt to forbid slavery in Missouri *did not result in the*

84

*freedom of one single slave.* The issue was where the slaves would be located. In fact, the Northern attempt to control "the expansion of slavery" was counter-productive and hostile to black people because de-concentrating the slave population over a larger territory would encourage ameliorated conditions and eventual emancipation.

When Thomas Jefferson looked westward he saw succeeding generations of Americans creating new self-governing commonwealths. If the future generations wanted to go off on their own and form new confederacies, which he expected to happen in the West, that was not a problem — they would still be Americans. He compared the new States to younger brothers who were free to go their own way. It was not the force of the federal government that held Americans together — it was their common blood and fellow feeling. The highest value was not a "sacred Union" but "consent of the governed."

When Lincoln's backers looked westward they had a very different vision. They saw natural resources to be exploited for private profit with government encouragement, new markets to be developed, more political offices to be filled, and a lure for thousands of immigrants to increase the value of the lands bestowed on the capitalists by the government — all enhancing the growing power of the "nation." For them the West was not a source of new self-governing States for Americans but a vast opportunity for wealth for those who knew how to grab the opportunity. And not a few Northerners were regarding the South in the same way. Southerners were not fellow Americans; they were troublesome obstacles to be got out of the way so that their territory could be properly exploited by "the nation." The War made this attitude widespread and respectable. From here it was only a short step to exterminating the obstacle. The same people who had tried to prevent the admission of Texas to the Union now regarded it not as a sister State worthy of respect but as a territory to be conquered and used. "Preserving the Union" now meant something very different from what it had before.[7]

Neither white nor black Southerners had any role to play in the new version of "the Union." One of the many ignored Northern realities of the time is that some Yankees expected the black population to die out when removed from the protection of slavery, and the white population to be exterminated or driven out. Then the South would be repopulated by New

Englanders who knew how to make maximum profit, using immigrants who were less expensive and more efficient workers than blacks. Some brilliant Yankee entrepreneurs thought they could take over plantations and produce the immensely valuable crops of the South more profitably than it was being done. A number followed in the wake of Union armies with the hope of getting rich on confiscated Southern plantations, and even more tried it during Reconstruction. Lots of Yankees got rich off the South during Reconstruction, but not from growing cotton.

Wall Street was already a major force in behalf of domestic operators and international bankers, all eager to "support" Lincoln's war. Any 21st century American who has not been asleep for the last few years is well aware how bankers thrive on government spending and debt.

In 1853 the Kansas-Nebraska acts were passed, killing the 1850 Compromise by allowing the question of slavery to be decided by the people of a Territory rather than by a geographic line, and raising a very slight possibility that there might be slavery above the Missouri Compromise Line. This was not done at the demand of Southerners, who indeed believed that only a sovereign State and not the people of a territory could decide this issue. The new and needless laws had to do with the schemes of Northern capitalists and politicians to expedite the construction of a transcontinental railroad from Chicago.

The Kansas-Nebraska acts created a backlash that brought together the agendas of many disparate elements of the North. They could all agree on an urgent need to prevent "the extension of slavery." Those who wanted to strike a blow at slavery, those who resented Southern political power that retarded Northern profits, New Englanders long bred on vicious hatred of everything Southern, people for whom the American Union must become a powerful unified "nation" with a unique holy mission, and those Northerners, numerous in every State, who feared having any black people near them, now all had a common platform. It was an issue which by his clever manipulation was to vault to prominence a seemingly washed-up but very clever and ambitious politician named Lincoln.

The resulting agitation fueled the rise of a new party, the Republicans. The Republicans made much of the Northwest Ordinance and the Missouri Compromise to suggest that their stand against "the extension of slavery," was a sacred policy of the Founding Fathers which vile Southerners were trying to overturn to spread their evil institution. They even named their party "Republican" after Jefferson's party. But their construction of the issue was pure dishonest demagoguery to arouse in the Northern public the belief that a diabolical "slave power conspiracy" was out to destroy the hallowed principles of the Founders. They were not copying Jefferson the critic of slavery, they were denying the Jefferson who had warned against raising a furor over "the extension of slavery." Not to mention that the Republicans stood for economic policies that were the polar opposite of Jeffersonian. The Republicans actually gave little thought to the effect of their propaganda on the South. Their goal was to embarrass and displace the Democratic Party in the North. That was Lincoln's strategy in his celebrated debates with Stephen A. Douglas in 1858.

A point that is nearly always hidden in discussions of the conflict over slavery: No Southerner ever insisted that any State, new or old, had to be a slave state. That was a matter that could only be settled by the sovereign people of a State itself. No Southern leader ever denied that a State could decide for itself whether to permit slavery. The Confederate Constitution allowed for the admission of non-slave States. The question was over the territories, not yet States, that were under the control of Congress and were the common inheritance of all citizens. The restriction of Southern settlement in new lands was an insult and a portent that the South faced an increasingly vulnerable status within the Union. As it become ever more evident that the North intended to dominate and rule in its own interests, Southerners began to insist increasingly that the North show good faith in obeying the Constitutional provisions in regard to slavery, about the only provisions left that favoured the South.

During the over-heated politics of the 1850s, Presidents Pierce and Buchanan and the Supreme Court all tried to encourage moderation and keep an even hand. But the aggressive new face of the North sensed triumph and would not be satisfied.

It is in this sense that the conflict leading up to secession was "about" slavery.

It is now established with almost Soviet rigour that the War to Prevent Southern Independence was "caused by" or "about" slavery. It is, in fact, absurd to attribute such an immense and revolutionary event to one cause. Earlier generations of historians, more objective and learned than the current crop, wrote about clashing economic interests and cultures and political ambitions and agitations as among the causes. The emphasis on slavery these days is not the result of some new historical wisdom or newly discovered truth. Rather it is the result of Americans today being obsessed with race and victimology, of the unfortunate tendency of many Americans to sugar-coat acts of aggression with idealistic rationalisations, and the cyclical intensification of the "blame the South" theme that has been chronic throughout American history.

Those who tout slavery as the whole and only cause of The War always cite the secession ordinances of the seven Deep South States that seceded first. Indeed, these did mention interference with slavery as one of the causes of separating from the Union. The current crop of historians have converted this one aspect into a blanket claim that the war was all about slavery, leaving an impression that it was entirely the South's fault for defending an evil institution against the benevolent agenda of the North for freedom. This makes the gigantic tacit and false assumption that the federal government had no choice about invading and destroying the South and that it did so to free the slaves.

Nothing could be more obvious than that the conflict over "the extension of slavery" was a contest of political power between the North and the South which had grown steadily apart in economics, religion, customs, values, and ways of life. According to a recent British historian, Marc Egnal: "For most Republicans nonextention [of slavery] was more an economic policy designed to secure Northern domination of Western lands than the initial step in a broad plan to end slavery." Though historians like to cite Lincoln's few pretty words about the immorality of slavery, the status and welfare of the African-American population carried no significant weight in the Republican agenda.

As Frederick Douglass, the leading black American of the 19th century, was later to observe, "Mr. Lincoln was pre-eminently the white man's president."[8]

The writer Ambrose Bierce, who was a hard-fighting Union soldier throughout the war, wrote that he had never met an abolitionist in the Union army and that the only black people he had seen were the concubines and servants of Union officers.

To assert that slavery was the sole "cause" of The War while ignoring the powerful driving force of the capitalists who adopted the Republican Party as their instrument, is superficial historianship and verges upon dishonesty. No serious observer can ignore this aspect. No honest thinker can accept any monocausal explanation for an event as huge and complex as the war of 1861-1865. Life is more complicated than that, and proper history teaches us about life.

Even if slavery in a sense was a cause of secession, it does not make it a cause of The War, for a war of conquest to prevent secession was a choice. And not an obvious one too many Northerners as well as Southerners. A choice made even more questionable by the fact of Lincoln's unprecedented election by only two-fifths of the people and the seceded States' declared willingness to negotiate in good faith. The South had no need to fight to "preserve slavery," which had long existed and was in no immediate peril. When the States declared that hostility to slavery was their reason for secession, they meant that they did not accept the right of ill-disposed, irresponsible outsiders to carry out an endless program of hateful slander and petty interferences with their daily life in a Union which their fathers and grandfathers had created for their liberty and well-being.

The "causes" of the war were many, but strictly speaking what the war was "about" was the nature of the Union. Black slaves had been an integral part of American (not just Southern) society for well over two centuries and nobody had gone to war either to keep them or to emancipate them. Indeed, Lincoln declared that he had neither the desire nor the power to interfere with slavery, and he would not know how to go about it even if he had the intent and the power. (Illinois did not admit black people to citizenship and sharply discouraged them from living there.)   Lincoln would not and could not inaugurate war to free the slaves. He could and did, however, inaugurate war.

As described in my previous article, a number of new developments were responsible for a hardening Northern attitude through the 1850s: One was the growing emotion of "national greatness," sometimes seen as a divine mission of a chosen people, the Americans. (Look at the lyrics of "The Battle Hymn of the Republic."). Nationalism, the desirability of one territory unified under one strong government, was a major idea in all the Western world in the 19th century and provided major support for the war against the South.   To this day it fuels the emotions of people who fervently but erroneously regard secession as "treason."

The influence of industrialists and bankers, which had been somewhat restrained by the interests of Northern traders and shippers, was now predominant.   Industry was strong and growing stronger. Chicago and Detroit had grown in barely a decade from hamlets to mighty industrial centers.   The new balance of power was revealed in 1860-1861 when the Southern-oriented free-traders of New York were vanquished by the Republicans.   Industry created a Northern proletariat of dependent workers for the first time in America, many of them foreign-born, who, among other things, could be persuaded to vote as their employers dictated and forced by unemployment or bribed by bounties to fill up the ranks of the Union armies.

Lincoln's party paid little attention to the status or welfare of African-Americans. They did however, as soon as they controlled Congress, pass:

1.   The highest tariff on imports in American history.
2.   A national banking system by which favoured institutions were entitled to create money out of the air and virtually control the credit and currency of the country (predecessor to the Federal Reserve).
3.   A massive giveaway of public lands which previously had been sold at modest prices to genuine settlers.   A popular plank of Lincoln's platform was "Vote Yourself a Farm," meaning a Homestead Law by which those who settled 160 acres of public land could own it.   But the real purpose of this law was to give away millions of acres of land to favoured railroad and mining interests.   It never occurred to the

emancipators to allow a single square inch of land in the great empty spaces of the Midwest to the freed slaves. That would be allowing them into Northern territory, to prevent which was a high priority for all nearly all Northerners, including the most avid opponents of slavery.

4. A contract labour law by which virtually enslaved gangs of foreign workers could be brought in — to keep down the wages of Native American labour.

5. A Morrill Act for "land-grant colleges" which inserted the federal government into education for the first time. Morrill, the Vermont Senator who was responsible for this legislation also gave his name to the "Morrill Tariff."

Not much to do with slavery, except that slavery helped to produce the immense crops of the South which made up the vast majority of America's foreign trade, which the ruling interests of the North were not about to relinquish. Chronology here is important, as it is, indeed, in achieving clarity about any historical event. Large segments of Northern opinion at first received secession calmly. "Let the erring sisters go in peace." Southerners, however rashly and unwisely, were simply invoking the good old American founding principle of "consent of the governed." Abolitionists felt freed of contamination. But then the capitalists began to collar the editors and the politicians. The North could not afford to let the highly productive Southern economy get beyond its grasp. Lincoln announced that he would initiate no hostilities but he would collect the tariff at the ports.[9]

Wall Street agreed and approved. Here is a private circular passed among bankers and brokers in late 1861:

Slavery is likely to be abolished by the war power and this. I and my friends are all in favor of, for slavery is but the owning of labor and carries with it the care of the laborers, while the European plan, led on by England, is that capital shall control labor by controlling wages. The great debt that capitalists will see to it is made out of the war must be used as a means to control the volume of money.

Quite true that Lincoln posed no immediate threat to slavery. That does not mean that he posed no threat to the South, however. Historians comb through every word uttered or written by Southerners at the time to identity evil and unworthy motives and are ingenious in explanations of why Southerners really meant something else more evil and devious than what they actually said. At the same time, Northern motives and actions are assumed as righteous on the basis of Lincoln's occasional pieties. On the one hand, Lincoln was the far-seeing and humane statesman who said that "a house divided against itself could not stand" and the nation must become all slave or all free. On the other hand, the South was hysterical in regarding this benevolent and moderate statesman as a threat. Lincoln is always allowed to have it both ways, as in the Gettysburg Address where he simultaneously claims credit for preserving the hallowed heritage of the founding fathers AND launching a revolutionary "new birth of freedom." Meanwhile, historians, most of them not even aware that they are doing so, always start with the assumption that Southerners are bad people who should not be viewed as having a single point on their side of the argument and whose words and acts must be reinterpreted to be seen in a negative light.

It is easy to believe in the honesty of Lincoln's position if you are already certain that Lincoln had been picked by God to lead the "nation" on to a higher plane. But very poor historianship to take Lincoln's words as conclusive without paying attention to the situation of the time. Abe was in fact covering his posterior and making things look good for European public opinion. Plenty of spokesmen for his party were at the same time boasting and crowing with delight that a Northern party was taking power that would serve Northern and only Northern interests.

Lincoln and respectable Republicans of course disclaimed John Brown. Brown, an obvious psychopath, in 1859 led a raid on a Virginia town and murdered a number of its citizens, including a respectable free black man and a grand-nephew of George Washington. (Brown wanted Washington's sword as a talisman.) He had pikes to arm the slaves and a constitution naming himself president. It is emblematic that Brown's raid is still celebrated as a "slave revolt," when in fact no slave had anything to do with it. Southerners understood perfectly that Brown's expedition was an attack by Northerners that it was financed and graced by some of the richest and most respectable

Yankees, and that in some quarters Brown's execution was proclaimed to be a noble martyrdom. A ludicrously false and sentimental painting showing Brown blessing a black baby on his way to the gallows shows how delusional much of Northern thinking about the South was.[10]

For the Republicans, widely regarded as radical troublemakers, to succeed to power Northerners had to be led to believe that the South was an actual threat to their way of life and values as well as to their economic interests. This impression Lincoln's party worked hard to implant. Relentless propaganda portrayed the South as a benighted land ruled by a few tyrannical aristocrats who lorded it over the slaves and a mass of degraded whites and conspired with Northern Democrats. To rule or ruin the Union and reduce the Northern working man to slavery. This slander was a false picture of the South, where democratic rule and rough social equality was as prevalent as in the North, if not more so. But the idea that Southern actions were explained by "a slave power," a conspiracy of a few aristocrats who completely dominated the South, was deeply implanted and is still invoked by historians who should know better. This false picture is essential to the moral justification of the Union cause. If the South was a democratic society in which the majority of the citizens made a free choice to separate from the North, their ruthless conquest seems far less righteous.

The Republican campaign against the non-existent "slave power conspiracy" reflects a common defense mechanism. Accuse others of the evil designs which you yourself entertain. And the false Republican claim that the South was dominated by a small aristocracy disguised the growing power of the wealthiest bankers and industrialists in the New York, a power that, unlike that of Southern leaders, was wielded behind the scenes, then and now. True, Southerners of all classes aspired to an aristocratic ideal of honourable behaviour, unlike pragmatic Yankees, but the South was as democratic as the North, any many ways more so. True, the South's democracy was only for white men, but in that respect it did not differ from the North.[11]

Thoughtful leaders of the South and eventually a large majority of the people saw secession as a way to avoid permanent economic exploitation and constant interference in their day-to-day life, which was likely to grow worse with the federal machinery in the hands of the first avowedly sectional party in American history. Northerners were determined to slander and harass the South relentlessly and replace the Union with a "nation" in their own image. All most Southerners wanted was to be left alone and for their one-time brethren of the North to stop abusing them at home and abroad. Further, thoughtful Southerners understood fully in 1860 that they had the strength of character, unique culture, and economic power to justify independence. Secession was no hysterical reaction and no conspiracy. Secession was openly and vigorously debated. The farewell speeches of Southern Senators in early 1861 are grave, calm, and sad.[12]

Republican rhetoric grew more heated and insulting as the 1850s moved on. Some Southerners replied in kind but most hoped that the uproar would die down as other mass enthusiasms in the North had. A few Southerners talked of re-opening the importation of slaves from Africa, but this was mostly a desire to tweak the Yankees' beaks. The idea never got any purchase and was quickly quashed by mainstream opinion. This same opinion ruled when the foreign slave trade was absolutely forbidden by the Confederate Constitution. A few Southerners talked of finding new slave states in the Caribbean or Central America. Most notably a soldier of fortune from Tennessee, William Walker, conducted a brief government in Nicaragua until the Yankee mogul Cornelius Vanderbilt had him murdered for interfering with his business.

These were ephemeral phenomenon that were frowned down by mainstream Southern opinion, but they provided "proof" to Republicans then and to historians later that there was a conspiracy underway by the leaders of the South to spread slavery.

Things reached critical proportions when men from Missouri and armed "settlers" from New England clashed over control of the territorial government of Kansas. Much of the violence was the usual frontier disorder and dispute over land claims, but some had to do with the sectional conflict. As far as the Northern press and subsequent historians are concerned, the whole thing was a question of Missouri ruffians beating up on saintly New England pioneers. This is very far from the truth. There was violence from both sides including Yankee atrocities against civilians in Missouri (which continued throughout The War and Reconstruction) and the stealing and mass murder endeavours of one of those saintly New Englanders, John Brown. Young William Quantrill, who came from Ohio to assist the antislavery forces, was so disgusted by their violence, greed, and hypocrisy that he joined the Southern side.[13]

"Bleeding Kansas" was the cause of the Brooks-Sumner incident. Senator Charles Sumner of Massachusetts, a pompous pseudo-intellectual disliked even by his allies, made a speech blaming Kansas troubles entirely on Southerners—a violent, criminal, unredeemable people unworthy of civilised company. He used such obscene language against South Carolina and her Senator Butler that several Northern Senators cried "Shame!" Sumner had previously announced that he would never participate in the barbarous Southern custom of dueling. So Representative Brooks of South Carolina, Butler's nephew and a veteran of the Mexican War, walked into the Senate when it was not in session and thrashed Sumner with a gutta-percha cane. Sumner feigned serious injury and spent most of the next two years in Europe, returning to the Senate only one day—to cast a vote for the tariff.[14]

The incident did not prove that Southerners were barbarians. What it proved was that America was now mentally and emotionally two different countries. Southerners, old-fashioned and serious people largely governed by a code of honour, believed that a man was responsible for his words. For many Northern leaders, politics was now a game. You said various things for various audiences to manipulate the voters and maneuver for advantage. Southerners did not understand this and Northerners did not understand that Southerners were serious men and not political gamesters.

This was proved decisively when Lincoln said from one side of his mouth that "a house divided against itself cannot stand" and the country must become all slave or all free. From the other side of his mouth he assured the South and moderate Northerners that he had not hostile intentions. His ambiguous stand was good politics in the North but even more threatening to the South than overt hostility. It would seem that in 1861 Lincoln believed that secession was merely political posturing and with a little show of strength he could overcome it. It was one of the most egregious mistakes in history.

More subtle, but perhaps more important, was the transformation of Northern politics into a business. Southern leaders sought office as they had always done, as a matter of honour and recognition. Increasingly Northern office-holders were party men, looking out for salaries and contracts. And generally second-class men subservient to the industrialists and bankers who wielded the real power without deigning to run for office. Historians have been quick to recognise and criticise the "Great Barbecue" of political/financial corruption that characterised the period after the war. Somehow, they seem to assume, this all mysteriously happened after the saintly Lincoln left the scene. In fact, the use of the government for profit in any and every way possible was intrinsic to the whole Republican agenda, Lincoln's war started it, and Lincoln was deeply involved in its practices.

The philosopher Orestes Brownson, a loyal but perceptive supporter of the Union, observed not long after the war:

> Nothing was more striking during the late civil war than the very general absence of loyalty or feeling of duty, on the part of the adherents of the Union.... The administration never dared confide in the loyalty of the federal people. The appeals were made to interest, to the democracy of the North against the aristocracy of the South; to anti-slavery fanaticism; or to the value and utility of the Union, rarely to the obligation in conscience to support the legitimate or legal authority; prominent civilians were bribed by high military commissions; others, by advantageous contracts for themselves or their friends for supplies to the army; and the rank and file by large bounties and high wages. There were exceptions, but such was the rule. [15]

There is another aspect of the history of "those people" of the North that historians have noted but avoided acknowledging the full significance of. Lincoln could not have won his election without foreigners and would have had a harder time winning his war if every fourth Union soldier had not been an immigrant. In the period before the war the South received some immigrants. It is a fact that almost every foreigner (and every Northerner too) who had lived in the South for any period of time before The War was a loyal Confederate. This tells us much about the hospitality and congeniality of Southern society, as does that fact that many Northern army officers who had married into Southern families resigned and joined the Confederacy.

By 1860 a fourth of the Northern population was made up of recent immigrants. Unlike the peaceful farmers who had come from Germany in the colonial period, those who came after 1848 were infected with Napoleonic militarism and revolutionary zeal. Between 1840 and 1860 the American white population increased by one-third from immigrants alone — including at least a million and a half Germans. They settled mainly in Lincoln's Midwest and made up from 8 to 17 per cent of the population of every Midwestern State in 1860. Lincoln recognised early the importance of this constituency to his ambitions by secretly purchasing a German language newspaper and subsidising several others. Recent German immigrants were prominent in the convention that nominated Lincoln and as Republican campaign orators. It appears that these immigrants tipped the balance, swinging the traditionally Democratic and Southern-oriented Midwest into the Republican column and making Lincoln's election possible. The civil war that broke out in Missouri at the beginning of The War resembled a fight between Confederate Americans and recently-arrived German Unionists.

The German revolutionaries brought with them an aggressive drive to realise in America the goals that had been defeated in their homeland with the failure of the revolutions of 1848. Their drive was towards "revolution and national unification," the slogan of the revolutionary Frankfurt Convention. The most prominent among them, Carl Schurz, shortly after his arrival, expressed disappointment at the non-ideological nature of American politics and vowed to change that. The Germans brought into the American regional conflict and into Republican rhetoric a diagnosis of class conflict (crusade to overthrow the "slave-drivers") and a spirit of militarism. This subverted the traditional moderate party politics of the Union.[16]

In January 1865 Karl Marx wrote an address in praise of Lincoln for an International Conference of Workers. Marx described the American war as a conflict between "the labour of the emigrant" and the aggression of the "slave driver." An evil rebellion, he said, had sprung up in the "one great democratic republic whence the first Declaration of the Rights of Man was issued." Marx knew nothing about America and even less about American labour and was applying abstract categories without meaning except to ideologues. But Marx took his cue from Lincoln in the Gettysburg Address in misrepresenting the Declaration of Independence as kin to the French Revolution's "Rights of Man." Marx's bankroller Friedrich Engels remarked: "Had it not been for the experienced soldiers who entered American after the European revolution, especially from Germany, the organization of the Union Army would have taken much longer than it did."[17]

Consider the enormity that Southern men, sons and grandsons of the founders of the country, fighting for their cherished self-government, are killed by foreigners in blue preaching an alien doctrine. Lincoln was not "preserving the Union" as he sometimes claimed, he was establishing an empire on a different model.

One of the best of Confederate memoirs is General Richard Taylor's *Destruction and Reconstruction.* In May 1865 Taylor went with one aide in a railroad handcar to find a ranking Union general and surrender the last few thousand Confederate soldiers in the vicinity of Mobile. Formalities concluded, the federal officers invited Taylor to join them for a meal (which he badly needed). Most of the federals behaved politely and avoided any conversation that would create hard feelings in their recently surrendered foe. However, as Taylor relates:

> There was, as ever, a skeleton at the feast, in the person of a general officer who had recently left Germany to become a citizen and soldier of the United States. This person, with the strong accent and idioms of the Fatherland, comforted me by assurances that we of the South would speedily recognise our ignorance and errors, especially about slavery and the rights of the States, and rejoice in the results of the war.... apologised meekly for my ignorance, on the ground that my ancestors had come from England to Virginia in 1608, and in the short intervening period of two hundred and fifty-odd years, had found no time to transmit to me correct ideas of the duties of American citizenship. Moreover, my grandfather, commanding the 9th Virginia regiment in our Revolutionary army, had assisted in the defeat and capture of the Hessian mercenaries at Trenton, and I lamented that he had not, by association with these worthies, enlightened his

understanding. My friend smiled blandly, and assured me of his willingness to instruct me.[18]

Taylor did not mention that he was the son of a President of the United States. "Those people" were triumphant, but they were a different people in a very different country from that of its Founders.

---

[1] The writings of the Virginian John Taylor of Caroline in the early 1800s are a comprehensive analysis of the Northern capitalist agenda and the inequities, deceptions, Constitutional distortions, and economic fallacies involved. Americans of the 21st century, suffering under catastrophic government debt and multi-billion dollar bailouts of bankers and speculators, could learn a lot from Taylor.

[2] For the tariff see *The Essential Calhoun,* ed. Clyde N. Wilson, (New Brunswick NJ: 1992), pp. 189-218.

[3] A Southerner invented the Gatling gun and the Colt revolver was designed by Texas Rangers. Confederate innovations in mines, artillery, ironclads, and submersibles are well-known. The Tar Heel genius Col. George W. Rains at the Augusta Arsenal made sure that the Southern army never lacked for gunpowder and small arms. The Italian historian Raimondo Luraghi has written the best history of Confederate industry, though not all of his works have been translated. Just before the 1860 election, a Yankee named Frederick Law Olmsted travelled through the South and published his observations in the Northern press. He is still cited by historians as evidence that the Southern population was ignorant, impoverished, surly, and backward, even though it is now known that Olmsted doctored his findings to make Republican Party propaganda.

[4]*Polk: The Diary of a President....* ed. Allan Nevins (New York: 1968), pp. 34-59.

5 Glover Moore, *The Missouri Controversy, 1819-1821* (Lexington KY: 1953)

6 Jefferson letters to John Holmes, April 22, 1820; to William Branch Giles, December 26, 1825.

7 Though unanimously hostile to the South, a number of historians have recently written candidly about Northern history in the period before and during the War to Prevent Southern Independence: Susan-Mary Grant, *North over South;* Harlow W. Sheidley, *Sectional Nationalism;* Richard F. Bensel, *Yankee Leviathan;*Ernest L. Tuveson, *Redeemer Nation; MarcEgnal, Clash of Extremes;* William Marvel, *Mr. Lincoln Goes to War.*

8 Frederick Douglass, "Oration in Memory of Abraham Lincoln," Washington, April 14, 1876.

9 Kenneth M. Stampp, *And the War Came . . .* (Baton Rouge: 1950); Charles Adams, *For Good and Evil . . .* (New York: 1992).

10 James C. Malin, *John Brown and the Legend of Fifty-Six* (Philadelphia: 1942); Otto J. Scott, *The Secret Six* (several editions).

11 Frank L. Owsley, *Plain Folk of the Old South,* is the classic description of the democratic society of the Old South. Though historians constantly repeat each other in stating that Owsley has been refuted, they can cite no substantial work that has done this, and recent historians, not sympathetic to the South but seeking a more complex picture, have supported Owsley.

12 *The Politics of Dissolution,* ed. Marshall L. DeRosa (New Brunswick NJ: 1998).

13 Paul R. Peterson, *Quantrill of Missouri: The Making of a Guerilla Warrior* (2003).

14 David H. Donald, *Charles Sumner and the Coming of the Civil War* (New York: 1960). Donald's biography of Charles Sumner is an illustration of how

American historians are affected by current events. In the first volume, cited above, Sumner is portrayed as a destructive figure. In the second volume, *Charles Sumner and the Rights of Man,* published in 1970, Sumner is a hero. Charles Sumner had not changed at all between 1960 and 1970, but the Civil Rights Revolution had got underway.

[15]*Orestes Brownson: Selected Political Essays,* ed. Russell Kirk (New Brunswick NJ: 1989), pp. 204-205

[16] Charlotte L. Brancaforte, ed., *The German Forty-Eighters in the United States* (New York: 1989); A.E. Zucker, ed., *The Forty-Eighters: Political Refugees of the German Revolution of 1848* (New York: 1950); Hans L. Trefousse, *Carl Schurz . . .* (Knoxville: 1982); Al Benson and Walter D. Kennedy, *Red Republicans and Lincoln's Marxists* (Gretna LA: 2011).

[17] Marx's manifesto is in *Abraham Lincoln: Selections from His Writings,* ed. Philip S. Foner, a Communist pamphlet published in New York in 1944.

[18] Richard Taylor, *Destruction and Reconstruction: Personal Reminiscences of the Civil War* (1879); pp. 230-231 in the 1998 J.S. Sanders edition.

# Shades of John Brown

SOUTHERNERS WHO HONOURtheir Confederate forebears have often been admonished: "Get over it. You lost!" The admonishers often do not follow their own advice. As a modest but earnest advocate of Southern heritage, I have quite often been threatened, usually anonymously, with harm to my person and a renewal of the extermination campaign against my people. I once received from Portland, Maine, a package containing a chamber pot labeled "Robert E. Lee's Soup Tureen." Not to mention the present hysteria which Paul C. Graham has aptly named "Confederaphobia."

Here is an interesting example from 1904. A woman named Blanche Boies entered the Kansas state capitol with an axe concealed under a cloak. She rode the elevator to the fifth floor headquarters of the Kansas Historical Society and proceeded to chop up a large picture of "Custer's Last Stand," a painting that had been commissioned by the Annheuser-Busch brewery of St. Louis,copies of which were at one time said to be in every tavern in America.

Asked to explain her actions, Ms. Boies said: "I concluded to chop the name of the secesh firm off, with no ,ill will toward the rest of the picture." This lady was a well-known follower of militant prohibitionist Carrie Nation. Somehow she thought that a Missouri brewer must have been secessionist, highly unlikely for St. Louis people with German names. And somehow she had associated the evil demon rum with the late Confederacy.

What she chopped was likely a copy. The original, for which a rather obscure artist was paid $30,000, seems to have been lost. Just a few years later Union and Confederate veterans met cordially on the field of Gettysburg and other                                                                                                  places.

# About the Author

DR. CLYDE WILSON is Distinguished Professor Emeritus of History of the University of South Carolina, where he served from 1971 to 2006. He holds a Ph.D. from the University of North Carolina at Chapel Hill. He recently completed editing of a 28-volume edition of *The Papers of John C. Calhoun* which has received high praise for quality. He is author or editor of more than a dozen other books and over 600 articles, essays, and reviews in a variety of books and journals, and has lectured all over the U.S. and in Europe, many of his lectures having been recorded online and on CDs and DVDs. Dr. Wilson directed 17 doctoral dissertations, a number of which have been published. Books written or edited include *Why the South Will Survive, Carolina Cavalier: The Life and Mind of James Johnston Pettigrew, The Essential Calhoun*, three volumes of *The Dictionary of Literary Biography* on American Historians, *From Union to Empire: Essays in the Jeffersonian Tradition, Defending Dixie: Essays in Southern History and Culture*, and *Chronicles of the South*.

Dr. Wilson is founding director of the Society of Independent Southern Historians; former president of the St. George Tucker Society for Southern Studies; recipient of the Bostick Prize for Contributions to South Carolina Letters, the first annual John Randolph Society Lifetime Achievement Award, and the Robert E. Lee Medal of the Sons of Confederate Veterans. He is M.E. Bradford Distinguished Professor of the Abbeville Institute; Contributing Editor of *Chronicles: A Magazine of American Culture;* founding dean of the Stephen D. Lee Institute, educational arm of the Sons of Confederate Veterans; and co-founder of Shotwell Publishing.

Dr. Wilson has two grown daughters, an excellent son-in-law, and two outstanding grandsons. He lives in the Dutch Fork of South Carolina, not far from the Santee Swamp where Francis Marion and his men rested between raids on the first invader.

# Available from Shotwell Publishing

---

*Maryland, My Maryland: The Cultural Cleansing of a Small Southern State* by Joyce Bennett (2016)

*Washington's KKK: The Union League During Southern Reconstruction* by John Chodes (2016)

*When the Yankees Come: Former South Carolina Slaves Remember Sherman's Invasion.* Edited with Introduction by Paul C. Graham (2016)

*Southerner, Take Your Stand!* by John Vinson (2016)

*Lies My Teacher Told Me: The True History of the War for Southern Independence* by Clyde N. Wilson (2016)

*Emancipation Hell: The Tragedy Wrought By Lincoln's Emancipation Proclamation* by Kirkpatrick Sale (2015)

*Southern Independence. Why War? - The War to Prevent Southern Independence* by Dr. Charles T. Pace (2015)

For more information, or to sign-up for notification of new releases, please visit

# ShotwellPublishing.com

98769569R00065

Made in the USA
Columbia, SC
06 July 2018